D1681829

AMERICAN HERITAGE

June, 1977 · Volume XXVIII · Number 4

© 1977 by American Heritage Publishing Co., Inc.
All rights reserved. Printed in the United States of America.

EDITOR
Alvin M. Josephy, Jr.

MANAGING EDITOR Geoffrey C. Ward
ART DIRECTOR Emma Landau
BOARD OF EDITORS
E. M. Halliday, *Chairman*
Bruce Catton, Barbara Klaw, Richard F. Snow, T. H. Watkins
PICTURE EDITORS
Devorah K. Cohen, Carla Davidson, Mary Dawn Earley
COPY EDITOR Brenda Savard
EDITORIAL ASSISTANTS
Elizabeth Oettinger, Mary Elizabeth Wise
PRODUCTION MANAGER Robin Ostrow
CONTRIBUTING EDITORS
Robert C. Alberts, Allan L. Damon,
Joan Paterson Kerr, Bernard A. Weisberger
ADVISORY BOARD
Henry Steele Commager,
Marshall B. Davidson, John A. Garraty,
Eugene D. Genovese, William H. Goetzmann,
Archibald Hanna, Howard H. Peckham,
Arthur M. Schlesinger, Jr.
CHIEF, EUROPEAN BUREAU Gertrudis Feliu
LONDON OFFICE Rosemary L. Klein

AMERICAN HERITAGE PUBLISHING COMPANY
CHAIRMAN OF THE BOARD
Samuel P. Reed
PRESIDENT AND PUBLISHER
Rhett Austell
EDITOR IN CHIEF—MAGAZINES
Alvin M. Josephy, Jr.
EXECUTIVE EDITOR—MAGAZINES
Nat Brandt
SENIOR EDITORS
Joseph J. Thorndike, Jr., Oliver Jensen
CONSULTING EDITOR
J. H. Plumb
EDITORIAL ART DIRECTOR Murray Belsky
TREASURER Anthony J. Sansiveri
PROMOTION DIRECTOR Ernest Quick
PROMOTION ART DIRECTOR David Van Inwegen
CIRCULATION AND SALES DIRECTOR Donald B. Barrows, Jr.
PRODUCTION DIRECTOR Elbert Burr

AMERICAN HERITAGE is published every two months by American Heritage Publishing Co., Inc.; editorial and executive offices, 10 Rockefeller Plaza, N.Y., N.Y. 10020. Secretary, Anthony J. Sansiveri. Correspondence about subscriptions should go to American Heritage Subscription Office, 383 West Center St., Marion, Ohio 43302. Single copies: $6. Annual subscriptions: $24 in U.S. and Canada; $26 elsewhere. A 10-year Index of Vols. VI-XV is available at $7.50; 5-year Index of Vols. XVI-XX at $7.50; 5-year Index of Vols. XXI-XXV at $7.50.

AMERICAN HERITAGE considers but assumes no responsibility for unsolicited materials; these require return postage. Title registered U.S. Patent Office. Second-class postage paid at New York, N.Y., and at additional mailing offices.

Postmaster: Please send Form 3579 to AMERICAN HERITAGE, 381 West Center Street, Marion, Ohio 43302.

AMERICAN HERITAGE has been selected by the Library of Congress for reproduction on recordings called Talking Books, distributed free by regional libraries in the U.S. to those unable to use conventional print because of a visual or physical handicap. For information write the Library of Congress, Division for the Blind and Physically Handicapped, 1291 Taylor St., N.W., Washington, D.C. 20542.

Mormon power: In 1886 The Wasp *of San Francisco lampooned the diligent, world-wide proselytizing efforts of the Church of Jesus Christ of Latter-day Saints. Rodman W. Paul's illuminating narrative, starting on page 74, shows how the Mormons grew—and why.*
BANCROFT LIBRARY, UNIVERSITY OF CALIFORNIA, BERKELEY

AMERICAN HERITAGE

THE MAGAZINE OF HISTORY

Sponsored by American Association for State & Local History · Society of American Historians

CONTENTS June, 1977 · Volume XXVIII · Number 4

FACES OF SLAVERY: A HISTORICAL FIND	4	*Elinor Reichlin*
AMERICA, EXPERIMENT OR DESTINY?	12	*Arthur M. Schlesinger, Jr.*
CARVING THE AMERICAN COLOSSUS	18	*E. M. Halliday*
THE FIRST FOURTH	28	*The 1777 celebration*
ORDEAL AT VELLA LAVELLA	30	*Walter Lord*
THE BIG THICKET	44	*A link with the frontier*
HIGH EAGLE: THE MANY LIVES OF TIM McCOY	52	*An interview by Darryl Ponicsan*
THE WAY I SEE IT	63	*Bruce Catton*
AMERICAN CHARACTERS: JOHN McLOUGHLIN	64	*David Lavender*
THE BUSINESSMAN AND THE GOVERNMENT	66	*John Brooks*
THE MORMONS: FROM PERSECUTION TO POWER	74	*Rodman W. Paul*
OUR MISPLACED PRESIDENT	84	*Andrew Ward*
THE IMPRISONMENT OF LAFAYETTE	86	*James Wesley Baker*
MOLE'S OTHER MASTERPIECES	92	*A photographic feature*
READERS' ALBUM: BIG BIRD	94	
CROSSWORD PUZZLE	95	*American sports*
BELLY-MY-GRIZZLE	96	*Spencer Klaw*
PRESERVING A NEIGHBORHOOD	106	
POSTSCRIPTS TO HISTORY	110	

COVER: The intriguing story of the sculpting of Mount Rushmore is told in an article beginning on page 18—but, in a way, the story is never quite finished, for the titanic stone faces have to be inspected and repaired every autumn. The repairs, performed by a workman who is something of an aerialist, are largely preventive; here, he operates on Lincoln's nose. Any new crack, however slight, is carefully filled with a mixture of granite dust, white lead, and linseed oil. This keeps water from seeping in, freezing, expanding, and producing more serious fissures. Photograph by courtesy of the South Dakota Division of Tourism.

The six previously unpublished daguerreotypes on the following pages represent an extraordinary historical find. Made in Columbia, South Carolina, in 1850 at the behest of Louis Agassiz, the celebrated father of American natural science, they are among the earliest known photographs of Southern slaves. So far as we know they are also the earliest for which the subjects are identified by name and by the plantation on which each one toiled. And, perhaps most remarkable, all but one of the slaves they depict were born in Africa, and three can be identified with the tribe or region from which they came. These pictures, part of a cache of fifteen, might have remained unknown had it not been for Elinor Reichlin, a former staff member of Harvard's Peabody Museum of Archaeology and Ethnology, who found them early last year in an unused storage cabinet in the museum's attic. Each daguerreotype case was embossed "J. T. Zealy, Photographer, Columbia" and several had handwritten labels. Nothing further was known about them. Ms. Reichlin spent months tracking down their story, and in the following article she explains just how and why these poignant images were made.

Faces of Slavery

Until the late 1830's, American scientists had little reason to question the Biblical explanation for mankind's racial diversity. They assumed that all men were descended from the sons of Noah, who had dispersed across the world as the waters of the Great Flood receded. Racial differences were the result of centuries spent in different climates.

Then, Dr. Samuel Morton, an eminent Philadelphia anatomist, published two books, *Crania Americana* (1839) and *Crania Aegypticus* (1844), which seemed to cast doubt on mankind's unity. After examining hundreds of ancient and modern skulls from both the Old World and the New, he noted that each region had been peopled by distinct races since antiquity. The Biblical time allotted to man's dispersal was far too short to account for such an ancient and extensive settlement of two widely separated continents by distinct races. Therefore, he reasoned, "mankind" must not be one species but several, each specially created by God to suit its own geographical environment.

Abolitionists decried Morton's theory; so did many religious persons, who considered it an attack on Scriptural truth. But it was eagerly seized upon by defenders of slavery who saw in it a "scientific" basis for racial inequality. The battle lines were drawn.

The most prestigious convert to the doctrine of separate creations was Louis Agassiz, who arrived from Switzerland in 1846, already persuaded from fossil studies that all animal species except man had been separately created and confined to the "zoological province" in which they lived. Talks with Morton and his followers helped convince Agassiz that the races, too, were different species. In March of 1850, before a meeting of the Association for the Advancement of American Science at Charleston, South Carolina, he declared that the races were "well marked and distinct" and did not originate "from a common center . . . nor from a common pair."

Special creationists were jubilant: ". . . with Agassiz in the war," wrote one, "the battle is ours." Their opponents were stunned. Agassiz was accused of unorthodoxy and was attacked for advocating slavery. Such assaults bewildered him; Agassiz was, in fact, deeply religious and largely indifferent to politics. Scientists, he believed, had a duty to search for truth wherever it led them, regardless of political and social consequences.

His method was to "study nature, not books," and after the Charleston meeting he traveled to Columbia to conduct field research on race. His host was Dr. Robert W. Gibbes, an admirer of Morton. Together, Gibbes and his illustrious guest traveled to nearby plantations where, Gibbes wrote, "Agassiz was delighted with his examinations of Ebo, Foulah, Gullah, Guinea, Coromantee, Mandrigo and Congo Negroes," and found enough

A slave daguerreotype, photographed in its case just as the author found it. The pinned label is in the handwriting of Dr. Robert W. Gibbes.

evidence to "satisfy him they have differences from other races." Agassiz concentrated exclusively on African-born slaves and their first-generation offspring. By means of this restricted sample he hoped both to define the anatomical variations unique to "the African race" in its original form and to establish a standard against which to measure the permanence of racial characteristics among American-born slaves of more remote African ancestry who had been exposed to a temperate climate for several generations. (African-born slaves in fact constituted only a tiny fraction of the U.S. slave population in 1850, more than four decades after Congress declared the importation of slaves illegal; some of those whom Agassiz examined must have been smuggled into America as part of the illicit trade that continued until the Civil War.)

His firsthand studies completed, Agassiz departed from Columbia at the end of March, but he evidently left instructions for Gibbes to gather corroborative photographic evidence—one of the first such instances in scientific history. Gibbes enthusiastically complied, arranging for J. T. Zealy to photograph the slaves Agassiz had examined, then posing each one nude to point up anatomical details in which the scientist had shown special interest and, finally, labeling each image with the subject's first name, tribe, and owner.

Gibbes was pleased with his work. "I have just finished the daguerreotypes for Agassiz of native Africans of various tribes," he wrote to Morton in June. "I wish you could see them."

Agassiz was probably satisfied as well; certainly his Columbia visit had reinforced his belief that Africans were a distinct species.

Although Agassiz never wavered in his belief, the theory of special creations was soon to be supplanted by the theory of evolution propounded by Charles Darwin in his *Origin of Species* (1859). Modern anthropologists, of course, are unanimous in their belief that mankind is a single species.

Agassiz' theory was discredited by the mid-1860's, but the daguerreotypes survived; and it is ironic that these pictures, made to demonstrate the supposed inferiority of their subjects, instead conferred a kind of immortality on the men and women we know only as Renty and Delia, Jem and Jack. It was no consolation for the humiliation they endured both as slaves and as objects of scientific curiosity, but a rare gain for those who now encounter these people as memorably real survivors of a painful epoch.

For further reading: Louis Agassiz: A Life in Science, *by Edward Lurie (University of Chicago Press, 1960), and* The Leopard's Spots, *by William Stanton (University of Chicago Press, 1960).*

Renty, an elderly field hand who lived on
B. F. Taylor's plantation, "Edgehill."
He is identified as a "Congo" slave.

Delia, Renty's daughter, was "countryborn of African parents." Her name appears along with her father's on an 1852 inventory of Taylor's slaves.

The identity of this man has long been lost.
The faint horizontal lines above his
waist appear to be ritual scarifications.

Jem, a "Gullah" slave owned by F. W. Green of
Columbia, South Carolina. Note the legs of the
headrest, used to hold subjects still for the camera.

Profile of Jack, a slave from the Guinea Coast. Ritual scars decorate his cheek.

Front view of Jack, who served as a
slave driver in B. F. Taylor's fields.

The New Man: An engraving after an 1852 sketch, The Night Watch, *by John W. Audubon*
YALE UNIVERSITY LIBRARY

AMERICA:
Experiment or Destiny?

by Arthur M. Schlesinger, Jr.

Nearly two centuries after Crèvecoeur propounded his notorious question—"What then is the American, this new man?"—Vine Deloria, Jr., an American Indian writing in the Bicentennial year on the subject "The North Americans" for *Crisis*, a magazine directed to American blacks, concluded: "No one really knows at the present time what America really is." Surely few observers were more entitled to wonder at the continuing mystery than those who could accurately claim the designation Original American. Surely no audience had more right to share the bafflement than one made up of descendants of slaves.

But we are all baffled by the meaning of the American experience. All any of us can do is descry a figure in the carpet—realizing as we do that contemporary preoccupations define our own definitions. My effort here will be to suggest two themes that seem to me to have subsisted in subtle counterpoint since the time when English-speaking white men first began the invasion of America. Both have dwelt within the American mind and struggled for its possession through the course of our history. Their competition will doubtless continue for the rest of the life of the nation. This essay aims to present these rival themes and to propose some points about the relationship between the divergent outlooks and the health of the republic.

I will call one theme the tradition and the other the countertradition, thereby betraying at once my own bias. The tradition, as I prefer to style it, sprang initially from historic Christianity as mediated by Augustine and Calvin. The Calvinist ethos was suffused with convictions of the depravity of man, of the awful precariousness of human existence, of the vanity of mortals under the judgment of a pitiless and wrathful deity. Harriet Beecher Stowe recalled the atmosphere in *Oldtown Folks:* "The underlying foundation of life ... in New England, was one of profound, unutterable, and therefore unuttered, melancholy, which regarded human existence itself as a ghastly risk, and, in the case of the vast majority of human beings, an inconceivable misfortune."

So terrible a sense of the nakedness of the human condition turned all of life into an unending and implacable process of testing. "We must look upon our selves," said William Stoughton, the chief justice of the court that condemned the Salem witches, "as under a *solemn divine Probation;* it hath been and it is a Probation-time, even to this whole People. . . ." So had it been at all times for all people. Most had failed the test. Were the American colonists immune to the universal law?

In the Calvinist view, all secular communities were finite and problematic; all flourished and all decayed; all had a beginning and an end. For Christians this idea had its *locus classicus* in the attempt to solve the problem of the decline and fall of Rome—a problem that transfixed the serious historical minds of the West from Augustine to Gibbon. By the time the revolutionaries came to Philadelphia in 1776, the flames of Calvinism were already burning low. Hell was dwindling into an epithet. Still, for the fathers of the republic as for the fathers of the church, the history of Rome remained the example from which they thought to learn the most about human possibilities.

COPYRIGHT © 1977 BY ARTHUR M. SCHLESINGER, JR.

From different premises, Calvinists and classicists reached the same conclusion about the fragility of human striving. Antiquity haunted the Federal imagination. The Founding Fathers had embarked on a singular adventure—the adventure of a *republic*. "The Roman republic," Alexander Hamilton wrote in the *Federalist*, "attained to the pinnacle of human greatness." In this conviction the first generation of the American republic designed its buildings, wrote its epics, named the upper chamber of its legislature, signed its greatest political treatise "Publius," sculpted its heroes in togas, organized the Society of the Cincinnati, and instructed the young. There was plausibility in the parallel. There was also warning. For the grandeur that was Rome had come to an inglorious end. Could the United States of America hope to do better?

The Founding Fathers passionately ransacked the classical historians for ways to escape the classical fate. But the classical indoctrination reinforced the Calvinist judgment that this was probation-time for America. For the history of antiquity did not teach the inevitability of progress. It proved rather the perishability of republics, the subversion of virtue by power and luxury, the transience of glory, the mutability of human affairs. The apprehension of the mortality of states was a vital element in the sensibility of Philadelphia in 1787. Not only was man vulnerable through his propensity to sin, but republics were vulnerable through their propensity to corruption. The dread of corruption, as Professor Bernard Bailyn has demonstrated, was readily imported from England to the colonies. History showed that, in the unceasing contest between corruption and virtue, corruption had always—at least up to 1776—triumphed.

The Founding Fathers had an intense conviction of the improbability of their undertaking. Such assets as they possessed came in their view from geographical and demographic advantage, not from divine intercession. Benjamin Franklin ascribed the inevitability of American independence to such mundane factors as population increase and vacant lands, not to providential design. But even these assets could not be counted on to prevail against history and human nature.

Hamilton said in the New York ratifying convention, "The tendency of things will be to depart from the republican standard. This is the real disposition of human nature." If Hamilton be discounted as a temperamental pessimist or a disaffected adventurer, his great adversaries were not always more sanguine about the republic's future. "Commerce, luxury, and avarice have destroyed every republican government," Adams wrote Benjamin Rush in 1808. ". . . We mortals cannot work miracles; we struggle in vain against the constitution and course of nature." "I tremble for my country," Jefferson had said in the 1780's, "when I reflect that God is just." Though he was trembling at this point—rightly and presciently—over the problem of slavery, he also trembled chronically in the nineties over the unlikely prospect of "monarchy." In 1798 he saw the Alien and Sedition Acts as tending to drive the states "into revolution and blood, and [to] furnish new calumnies against republican government, and new pretexts for those who wish it to be believed, that man cannot be governed but by a rod of iron."

This pervasive self-doubt, this urgent sense of the precariousness of the national existence, was no doubt nourished by European assessments of the American prospect. For eminent and influential Europeans regarded the New World, not as an idyl of Lockean felicity—"in the beginning, all the world was America"—but as a disgusting scene of degeneracy and impotence.

In the middle of the eighteenth century, the famous Buffon lent the weight of scientific authority to the proposition that life in the Western Hemisphere was consigned to biological inferiority. American animals were smaller and weaker; European animals shrank when transported across the Atlantic, except, Buffon specified, for the fortunate pig. As for the natives of the fallen continent, they too were small and weak, passive and backward.

No one made this case more irritatingly and perseveringly than Abbé Raynal in France. His much-reprinted work, *Philosophical and Political History of the Settlements and of the Commerce of Europeans in the Two Indies,* first published in 1770, explained how European innocence was under siege by American depravity. America, Raynal wrote, had "poured all the sources of corruption on Europe." The search for American riches brutalized the European intruder. The climate and soil of America caused the European species, human as well as animal, to deteriorate. "The men have less strength and less courage . . . and are but little susceptible of the lively and powerful sentiment of love"—a comment that perhaps revealed Raynal in the end more as a Frenchman than as an abbé.

The Founding Fathers were highly sensitive to the proposition that America was a mistake. Franklin, who thought Raynal an "ill-informed and evil-minded Writer," once endured a monologue by the diminutive abbé on the inferiority of the Americans at his own dinner table in Paris. "Let us try this question by the fact before us," said Franklin, calling on his guests to stand up and measure themselves back to back. "There was not one American present," wrote Jefferson, who was also there, "who could not have tost out of the Windows any one or two of the rest of the Company."

Though the Founders were both indignant and effective in their rebuttal, the nature of the attack could hardly have increased their confidence in the future of their adventure. The European doubt, along with the Calvinist judgment and the classical pessimism, made them acutely aware of the chanciness of an extraordinary enterprise. From the fate of the Greek city-states and the fall of the Roman Empire, they drew somber conclusions about the prospects of the American republic. They had no illusions about the inviolability of America to history, nor about the perfectibility of man, Americans or others. The Constitution, James Bryce has well said, was "the work of men who believed in original sin, and were resolved to leave open for transgressors no door which they could possibly shut."

We have all applied the phrase "end of innocence" to one or another stage of American history. This is surely an amiable flourish—or a pernicious delusion. No people who systematically enslaved black men and killed red men could be innocent. No people reared on Calvin and Tacitus, on Jonathan Edwards and the *Federalist,* could be innocent. No nation founded on invasion, conquest, and slaughter could be innocent. No state established by revolution and thereafter rent by civil war could be innocent. The Constitution was hardly the product of immaculate conception. The Founding Fathers were not a band of saints. They were brave and imperturbable realists who committed themselves, in defiance of the available lessons of history and theology, to a monumental gamble.

This is why Hamilton, in the third sentence of the first *Federalist,* formulated the issue as he did. The American people, he wrote, had the opportunity "by their conduct and example, to decide the important question, whether societies of men are really capable or not of establishing good government from reflection and choice, or whether they are forever destined to depend for their political constitutions on accident and force." So Washington defined it in his first Inaugural Address: "The preservation of the sacred fire of liberty and the destiny of the republican model of government are justly considered, perhaps, as *deeply,* as *finally,* staked on the experiment intrusted to the hands of the American people." The Founding Fathers saw the American republic not as a consecration but as the test against history of a hypothesis.

Washington's early successors, with mingled anxiety and hope, reported on the experiment's fortunes. In his last message to Congress, James Madison permitted himself "the proud reflection that the American people have reached in safety and success their fortieth year as an independent nation." "Our institutions," said James Monroe in his last message, "form an important epoch in the history of the civilized world. On their preservation and in their utmost purity everything will depend." Washington, said Andrew Jackson in his own Farewell Address, regarded the Constitution "as an experiment" and "was prepared to lay down his life, if necessary, to secure to it a full and a fair trial. The trial has been made. It has succeeded beyond the proudest hopes of those who framed it." "The present year," Martin Van Buren said in 1838, "closes the first half century of our Federal institutions.... It was reserved for the American Union to test the advantages of a government entirely dependent on the continual exercise of the popular will." "After an existence of near three-fourths of a century as a free and independent Republic," said Polk in the next decade, "the problem no longer remains to be solved whether man is capable of self-government." Sixty years after the Constitution, Zachary Taylor pronounced the United States of America "the most stable and permanent Government on earth."

How is one to account for this rising optimism? It was partly a tribute, reasonable enough, to survival. It was partly the spread-eagleism and vainglory congenial to a youthful nationalism. It was no doubt also in part admonitory exhortation, for the Presidents of the middle period must have known in their bones that the American experiment was confronting its fiercest internal trial. No one understood more profoundly the chanciness of the adventure than the young man who spoke in 1838 on "The Perpetuation of our Political Institutions" before the Young Men's Lyceum of Springfield, Illinois. Over most of the first half century, Abraham Lincoln said, America had been felt "to be an undecided experiment; now, it is understood to be a successful one." But success contained its own perils; "with the catching, end the pleasures of the chase." As the memory of the Revolution receded, the pillars of the temple of liberty were crumbling away. "That temple must fall, unless we ... supply their places with other pillars, hewn from the solid quarry of sober reason." The conviction of the incertitude of life informed his Presidency—and explained its greatness. His first message to Congress asked whether all republics had an "inherent and fatal weakness." At the Gettysburg cemetery he described the great civil war as "testing" whether any nation conceived in liberty and dedicated to the proposition that all men are created equal "can long endure."

This was, then, a dominant theme of the early republic—the idea of America as an experiment, undertaken in defiance of history, fraught with risk, problematic in outcome. But a countertradition was also emerging—and, as the mounting presidential optimism suggests, with accumulating momentum. The countertradition, too, had its roots in the Calvinist ethos.

Historic Christianity embraced two divergent thoughts: that all people were immediate unto God; and that some were more immediate than others. At first, Calvin had written in the *Institutes,* God "chose the Jews as his very own flock." Then, with what Edwards called "the abolishing of the *Jewish dispensation,*" the wall was "broken down to make way for the more extensive success of the gospel." The chosen people thereafter were the elect as against the reprobate. The age that sent the Calvinists to New England also saw a revival of the primitive millennialism of the first century. The New Englanders felt they had been called from hearth and home to endure unimaginable rigor and ordeal in a dangerous land; so they supposed someone of importance had called them, and for important reasons. "God hath covenanted with his people," said Increase Mather, "that sanctified afflictions shall be their portion.... *Without doubt, the Lord Jesus hath a peculiar respect unto this place, and for this people.*"

It was not only that they were, in Winthrop's words, as a City upon a Hill, with the eyes of all people upon them. It was that they had been despatched to New England, as Edward Johnson said, by a Wonder-working Providence because "this is the place where the Lord will create a new Heaven, and a new Earth." The "Lord Christ" intended "to make his *New England* Souldiers the very wonder of this Age." The fact that God had withheld America so long—until the Reformation purified the church, until the invention of printing spread the Bible among the people—argued that He had been preparing it for some ultimate manifestation of His grace. God, said Winthrop, having "smitten all the other Churches before our eyes," had reserved America for those whom He meant *"to save out of this generall callamitie,"* as he had once sent the ark to save Noah. The new land was certainly a part, perhaps the climax, of redemptive history; America was divine prophecy fulfilled.

The achievement of independence gave new status to this theory. The Reverend Timothy Dwight, Jonathan Edwards' grandson, called Americans "this chosen race." "God's mercies to New England," wrote Harriet Beecher Stowe, daughter of one minister, wife of another, foreshadowed "the glorious future of the United States . . . commissioned to bear the light of liberty and religion through all the earth and to bring in the great millennial day, when wars should cease and the whole world, released from the thralldom of evil, should rejoice in the light of the Lord." "We Americans," wrote the youthful Herman Melville, "are the peculiar, chosen people—the Israel of our time; we bear the ark of the liberties of the world. . . . Long enough have we been skeptics with regard to ourselves, and doubted whether, indeed, the political Messiah had come. But he has come in *us.*"

The belief that Americans were a chosen people did not imply a sure and tranquil journey to salvation. As the Bible made amply clear, chosen people underwent the harshest trials and assumed the most grievous burdens. The rival propositions—America as experiment, America as destiny—thus shared a belief in the process of testing. But one proposition tested works; the other, faith. So Lincoln and Mrs. Stowe agreed from different standpoints in seeing the Civil War as the climactic test. Northern victory, however, strengthened the conviction of providential appointment. "Now that God has smitten slavery unto death," Mrs. Stowe's brother Edward wrote in 1865, "he has opened the way for the redemption and sanctification of our whole social system."

It was a short step from the Social Gospel at home to Americans carrying the Social Gospel to the world. In 1898 the Reverend Alexander Blackburn, who had been wounded at Chickamauga, spoke of "the imperialism of righteousness"; and from Blackburn to the messianic demagoguery of Albert J. Beveridge was only another short step: "God has not been preparing the English-speaking and Teutonic peoples for a thousand years for nothing but vain and idle self-contemplation. . . . And of all our race He has marked the American people as His chosen nation to finally lead in the regeneration of the world."

So the impression developed that in the United States of America the Almighty had contrived a nation unique in its virtue and magnanimity, exempt from the motives that governed all other states. "America is the only idealistic nation in the world," said Woodrow Wilson on his pilgrimage to the West in 1919. ". . . The heart of this people is pure. The heart of this people is true. . . . It is the great idealistic force of history. . . . I, for one, believe more profoundly than in anything else human in the destiny of the United States. I believe that she has a spiritual energy in her which no other nation can contribute to the liberation of mankind. . . ."

In another forty years the theory of America as the savior of the world received the furious imprimatur of John Foster Dulles, another Presbyterian elder, and from there roared on to the horrors of Vietnam. So the hallucination brought the republic from the original idea of America as exemplary experiment to the recent idea of America as mankind's designated judge, jury, and executioner. Nor are we yet absolutely clear that the victor in the Bicentennial election may not believe that nations, like Presidents, may be born again.

Why did the conviction of the corruptibility of men and the vulnerability of states—and the consequent idea of America as experiment—give way to the myth of innocence and the delusion of a sacred mission and a sanctified destiny? The original conviction was rooted in realistic conceptions of history and of human nature—conceptions that waned as the republic prospered. The intense historical-mindedness of the first generation did not endure. "The Past," Melville said in *White Jacket,* "is dead, and has no resurrection; but the Future is endowed with such a life that it lives to us even in anticipation." The new nation was largely populated by people torn from, fleeing from, or in revolt against their own histories. "Probably no other civilised nation," said the *Democratic Review* in 1842, "has . . . so completely thrown off its allegiance to the past as the American."

We find ourselves now, for all the show-business clatter of the Bicentennial celebrations, an essentially historyless people. Businessmen agree with the elder Henry Ford that history is bunk. The young no longer study history. Intellectuals turn their backs on history in the enthusiasm for the ahistorical behavioral "sciences." As the American historical consciousness has thinned out, the messianic hope has flowed into the vacuum. Experiment has given ground to destiny as the premise of national life.

So the theory of the elect nation, the redeemer nation, the happy empire of perfect wisdom and perfect virtue, almost became the official creed. Yet, while the countertradition prospered, the tradition did not quite expire. Some continued to regard it all as the deceitful dream of a golden age, wondering perhaps why the Almighty should have chosen the Americans. "The Almighty," Lincoln insisted at his second Inaugural, "has His own purposes." He clearly knew what he was saying, because he wrote soon thereafter to a fellow ironist, Thurlow Weed: "Men are not flattered by being shown that there has been a difference of purpose between the Almighty and them. To deny it, however . . . is to deny that there is a God governing the world."

After the war, Walt Whitman, once the supreme poet of democratic faith, suddenly perceived a dark and threatening future. The experiment was in jeopardy. These States, no longer a sure thing, were caught up in a "battle, advancing, retreating, between democracy's convictions, aspirations, and the people's crudeness, vice, caprices." America, Whitman apprehended, might well "prove the most tremendous failure of time." "'Tis a wild democracy," Emerson said in his last public address; "the riot of mediocrities and dishonesties and fudges." A fourth generation of Adamses raised particularly keen doubts whether

Providence in settling America had after all opened a grand design to emancipate mankind. Henry Adams began as a connoisseur of political ironies; later he became a sort of reverse millennialist, convinced that science and technology were rushing the planet toward an apocalypse unredeemed by a Day of Judgment. "At the rate of increase of speed and momentum, as calculated on the last fifty years," he wrote in 1901, "the present society must break its damn neck in a definite, but remote, time, not exceeding fifty years more." The United States, like everything else, was finished. In the end Adams too abandoned experiment for destiny; but destiny for him was not only manifest but malign. "No one anywhere," he wrote a few weeks before the outbreak of the First World War, ". . . expects a future."

William James, the philosopher, retained the experimental faith, abhorring the fatalisms and absolutes implied by "the idol of a national destiny . . . which for some inscrutable reason it has become infamous to disbelieve in or refuse." We are instructed, James said, "to be missionaries of civilization. . . . We must sow our ideals, plant our order, impose our God. The individual lives are nothing. Our duty and our destiny call, and civilization must go on. Could there be a more damning indictment of that whole bloated idol termed 'modern civilization'?" All this had come about too fast "for the older American nature not to feel the shock." One cannot know what James meant by "the older American nature"; but he plainly rejected the supposition that American motives were, by definition, pure; and that the United States enjoyed a divine immunity to temptation and corruption. Like the authors of the *Federalist,* James was a realist. "Angelic impulses and predatory lusts," he precisely wrote, "divide our heart exactly as they divide the heart of other countries."

So the warfare between realism and messianism, between experiment and destiny, continued to our own day. If some political leaders were messianists, the perception of America as an experiment conducted by mortals of limited wisdom and power without divine guarantee informed the practical intelligence of others. The second Roosevelt saw life as uncertain and the national destiny as problematic. The republic was still an experiment and "demands bold, persistent experimentation. It is common sense to take a method and try it: If it fails, admit it frankly and try another. But above all, try something." Roosevelt's realism kept American participation in the Second World War closer to a sense of national interest than of world mission. In a later time John Kennedy argued that antimessianic case: "We must face the fact that the United States is neither omnipotent nor omniscient—that we are only 6 per cent of the world's population—that we cannot impose our will upon the other 94 per cent of mankind—that we cannot right every wrong or reverse each adversity—and that therefore there cannot be an American solution to every world problem." "Before my term has ended," he said in his first annual message, "we shall have to test anew whether a nation organized and governed such as ours can endure. The outcome is by no means certain."

This evoked the mood of the Founding Fathers. But the belief in national righteousness and providential destiny remains strong—a splendid triumph of dogma over experience. One cannot but feel that this belief has encouraged our recent excesses in the world and that the republic has lost much by forgetting what James called "the older American nature." For messianism is an illusion. No nation is sacred and unique, the United States or any other. All nations are immediate unto God. America, like every country, has interests, real and fictitious; concerns, generous and selfish; motives, honorable and squalid. Providence has not set Americans apart from lesser breeds. We too are part of history's seamless web.

Yet we retain one signal and extraordinary advantage over most nations—an entirely secular advantage, conferred upon us by those quite astonishing Founding Fathers. For they bequeathed us standards by which to set our course and judge our performance—and, since they were exceptional men, the standards have not been rendered obsolete even by the second law of thermodynamics. The Declaration of Independence and the Constitution establish goals, imply commitments, and measure failures. The men who signed the Declaration, said Lincoln, "meant to set up a standard maxim for a free society, which should be familiar to all, and revered by all; constantly looked to, constantly labored for, and even though never perfectly attained, constantly approximated, and thereby constantly spreading and deepening its influence, and augmenting the happiness and value of life to all people of all colors everywhere."

We can take pride in our nation, not as we pretend to a commission from God and a sacred destiny, but as we struggle to fulfill our deepest values in an inscrutable world. As we begin our third century, we may well be entering our golden age. But we would be ill advised to reject the apprehensions of the Founding Fathers. Indeed, a due heed to those ancient anxieties may alone save us in the future. For America remains an experiment. The outcome is by no means certain. Only at our peril can we forget the possibility that the republic will end like Gatsby in Scott Fitzgerald's emblematic fable—Gatsby who had come so long a way and whose "dream must have seemed so close that he could hardly fail to grasp it. He did not know that it was already behind him, somewhere back in that vast obscurity beyond the city, where the dark fields of the republic rolled on under the night.

"Gatsby believed in the green light, the orgastic future that year by year recedes before us. It eluded us then, but that's no matter—tomorrow we will run faster, stretch out our arms farther. . . . And one fine morning—

"So we beat on, boats against the current, borne back ceaselessly into the past."

Arthur M. Schlesinger, Jr., is Schweitzer Professor of Humanities, City University of New York, and the author of many distinguished historical studies. His essay is adapted from a paper read at a meeting of the American Historical Association last December.

18

Carving the American Colossus

The granite was tough – but so was Gutzon Borglum

by E. M. Halliday

Opposite: Individual photos of Mount Rushmore's four heads, taken as each neared completion, suggest that the "carving" was as much a matter of engineering as of art. Clockwise from upper left: Theodore Roosevelt (dedicated in 1939); George Washington (1930); Thomas Jefferson (1936); Abraham Lincoln (1937). Men are at work on all except Washington.
ALL: SOUTH DAKOTA DIVISION OF TOURISM

In late August, 1970, a band of Sioux Indians entered the sacred precincts of a National Memorial in South Dakota and bivouacked on a mountaintop there for several weeks. The precincts were sacred to the Sioux because they are in the heart of the Black Hills, long regarded by their tribe as the dwelling place of Indian gods and spirits. And, as signaled by the apprehensive behavior of park rangers who monitored the Indians closely during their stay, the precincts are also precious to the United States Department of the Interior. For there, looming high above the valley floor, gazing off across hundreds of miles of the South Dakota Badlands, are the gigantic stone faces of Washington, Jefferson, Lincoln, and Theodore Roosevelt hewn from the primeval granite by sculptor Gutzon Borglum in fourteen years of labor on precipitous Mount Rushmore.

The Indians wanted Mount Rushmore "back," as they put it. What they meant, they explained, was that the entire Black Hills area was guaranteed as Indian territory by the Treaty of Fort Laramie in 1868—a treaty spectacularly ignored after an expedition led by George Armstrong Custer found gold in 1874. They thought it was high time for the government to make some modest compensation for that enormous treaty violation. Beyond that, they were not happy with a monument that celebrates the founding of the white man's nation (Washington), the acquisition of vast tracts of Indian hunting and living space without regard to Indian wishes (Jefferson), and the consolidation and expansion of the intruders' domain into the most powerful sovereignty in the world (Lincoln and Roosevelt). "They could just as well have carved this mountain into a huge cavalry boot standing on a dead Indian," one of the Indians said later.

The Sioux invaders found a comfortable campsite up behind Teddy Roosevelt's skull, painted "RED POWER" on a nearby expanse of rock, and settled in with food and water transported to them regularly by local compatriots. They did not, as the rangers had feared they might,

19

pour red paint over the great presidential noses or otherwise mutilate the monument; but they did succeed in attracting considerable regional and national attention to the situation of the American Indian today, and in engendering among many people second thoughts about the meaning of Mount Rushmore in the national iconology.

The whole episode would have been deeply disturbing to Gutzon Borglum, who counted himself a close friend of the Sioux, and who despite his foreign-sounding name was almost egregiously American, born in Idaho in 1867 and raised in Nebraska and California. Mount Rushmore was by far his most heroic undertaking—heroic in its proportions, its difficulties, and its artistic symbolism—and he always felt intensely about its import as American mythology. "There on the mountain top," he wrote in 1940, "as near to Heaven as we could make it, we have carved portraits of our leaders, that posterity and civilization may see hundreds of thousands of years hence what manner of men our leaders were, with a prayer and a belief that there among the clouds they may stand forever, where wind and rain alone shall wear them away."

Although Borglum had long wanted to sculpt a mountain into a great monument, and in fact had already developed considerable skill as a mountain carver in Georgia, the idea of such a project in the Black Hills was not originally his. It came from Doane Robinson, for many years the state historian of South Dakota and a well-known writer on Western history. In 1923 Robinson had been contemplating the Black Hills Needles, great spires of solid granite that are the residual cores of mountain peaks long since eroded away, and it struck him that some of them might be carved into tremendous historical statues. "In my imagination," he said, "I can see all the old heroes of the west peering out . . . Lewis and Clark, Frémont, Jed Smith, Bridger, Sa-kaka-wea, Red Cloud, and in an equestrian statue, Cody and the overland mail." Inspired by this heady vision, Robinson sought public support for his idea. The much respected South Dakota senator Peter Norbeck was sympathetic, as were a few regional newspaper editors; but others sputtered about tampering with "nature's handiwork." "Man makes statues but God made the Needles," announced the Hot Springs *Star;* "Let them alone."

The undaunted Robinson had heard about Gutzon Borglum's work on Stone Mountain, Georgia, a few miles from Atlanta. There, after a series of troublesome fits and starts, the sculptor had begun a bas-relief high up on the side of the mountain, depicting Robert E. Lee and other Confederate leaders riding into history in glorious defeat; his twenty-foot head of Lee had been unveiled on January 19, 1924. Here was a man who clearly knew how to carve granite on a titanic scale, and Robinson wrote Borglum suggesting "a massive sculpture" in the Black Hills. He was unaware that the artist was having ferocious troubles with the Stone Mountain Monumental [*sic*] Association over the administration of the project, and was delighted when, late in September, 1924, Borglum arrived to look over the terrain. Accompanied by his twelve-year-old son, Lincoln Borglum, as well as by historian Robinson and a few local enthusiasts, the sculptor toured beautiful Custer State Park and the next day climbed Harney Peak, the highest (7,242 feet) in the Black Hills. He was more than impressed by what he saw from that eminence. Nearby and in the distance rose an array of granite needles and outcroppings that seemed to him to beg for sculpting. "There's the place to carve a great national memorial," Doane Robinson reported him as saying. "American history shall march along that skyline!"

This somewhat majestic rhetoric was pure Borglum, for he was a man not given to understatement. It also hinted that the sculptor would not be content to carve figures of Western or regional heroes; he wanted a truly national monument, and proposed Washington and Lincoln as obviously appropriate candidates. Senator Norbeck was not happy with what he called Borglum's "Washington-Lincoln Siamese twins idea," and on thinking it over, the artist himself concluded that "making totem poles of these wonderful spires [the Needles]" was indeed the wrong approach. Instead, "we want to go back into the Hills, find some now unknown massive stone, and carve these figures upon them."

In August, 1925, Borglum found his "unknown massive stone." He had been guided by a state forester into a remote area of the Harney National Forest where there were more extensive outcroppings than the Needles offered. About three miles northeast of Harney Peak, Borglum came to a halt, staring with a wild surmise at an enormous expanse of weathered gray stone, seamed with wrinkles and fissures across its nearly perpendicular side, but apparently one solid mass of granite underneath. Crowding the sky at six thousand feet, it looked like the body of a huge prehistoric elephant that had become petrified in some cataclysmic episode millions of years ago. Borglum felt immediately that this was his mountain, and quickly sketched it—with a head of Washington roughed in against the granite side near the top.

The artist learned that this extraordinary mountain was called Rushmore—casually named in 1885 after Charles E. Rushmore, a New York lawyer who was struck by its appearance when he encountered it on a trip to check property titles for miners in the area. Although Borglum conscientiously examined other stone masses in the vicinity, the more he studied Mount Rushmore the more he grew convinced that this was the right place for the singular monument he had in mind. The granite, although rugged—geologists guessed it would erode at a rate not faster than an inch in 100,000 years—seemed suitably grained for accurate cutting; the posture of the mountain was perfect in terms of natural lighting, for its most carvable surface faced southeast and would be bathed in sunlight nearly all day.

Legislation to permit mountain sculpture in the Black Hills had already been passed by Congress and

Gutzon Borglum, the sculptor, spent thousands of hours on the side of Mount Rushmore directing the carving of the monument.
SOUTH DAKOTA DIVISION OF TOURISM

by the South Dakota state legislature. Borglum exhibited a distinctly Barnumesque flair in working up plans for dedication of the chosen site, and after lively publicity a couple of thousand citizens hiked out to the base of Mount Rushmore on October 1, 1925. There they watched performers in costume—Indian, French, Spanish, English, and American, to indicate successive "ownership"—go through a fancy flag-raising ceremony atop the mountain, and heard Borglum declare sonorously that if they would come back in a year they would see the finished head of George Washington that was (as he liked to put it) waiting in the granite to be released.

In fact, two years went by before carving was even begun on Mount Rushmore. The chief problem was one from which the project was never to be free: lack of money. Borglum, who lived lavishly but was almost always in debt, tended to assume that the patriotic appeal of the proposed monument, enhanced by skillful promotion, would bring forth large sums from both public and private sources. Events revealed instead a skeptical reluctance in Congress to appropriate funds for Rushmore, and an almost incredible parsimony on the part of the state of South Dakota, which never appropriated a dime for what was eventually to become its most popular tourist attraction. Private contributions ran to dribbles rather than floods. It was, to be sure, an expensive business by the frugal standards of the time: in the end—1941—the total outlay for Mount Rushmore would be calculated at $989,992, of which federal appropriations accounted for $836,000.

While the Mount Rushmore enterprise got off to a halting start, Gutzon Borglum managed, as always, to keep unflaggingly busy. A few months before the dedication in the Black Hills he had brought his connection with the Stone Mountain Monumental Association to a literally crashing conclusion by pushing his plaster models over the side of the cliff after discovering that he had just been dismissed for insubordination and mismanagement; he then hastily departed for points north while Georgia lawmen tried to catch him before he crossed the border. The disastrous Stone Mountain episode had not been without its instructive aspects, however. Borglum had learned some clever techniques of mountain carving that would be essential on Mount Rushmore; and the South Dakotans who would be involved with the production of the monument had learned that they were dealing with a man who had all the traditional characteristics of the temperamental artist, and then some. They even received a helpful brochure from the Stone Mountain association describing Borglum as greedy, truant, unreliable, offensively egotistical, and possessed by delusions of grandeur.

Such charges were no news to Borglum. In 1925, in his fifty-ninth year, the bald but fiercely mustachioed artist was one of America's most widely known sculptors, as much for his bumptious personality as for his great productivity. His early years in art had followed a familiar pattern: encouragement by older American artists, a few years of study in Paris (during which he became a disciple of Auguste Rodin), shows and commissions back in the States and in London. At first successful as a painter, he veered steadily toward sculpture after 1904, when he won a gold medal at the St. Louis Exposition for his equestrian *Mares of Diomedes*.

21

Certain subjects in American history particularly intrigued Borglum, among them Abraham Lincoln. His treatment was habitually realistic. "I think it is the most extraordinarily good portrait of my father I have ever seen," said Robert Lincoln after the sculptor chiseled a head of the Emancipator out of a three-foot block of marble in 1908. (It now stands in the Capitol Rotunda.) Borglum did a big mounted statue of General Philip Sheridan for Washington, D.C., and in 1911 another larger-than-life Lincoln—this time full length—for the courthouse in Newark, New Jersey, which won a bully tribute from Teddy Roosevelt: "This doesn't look like a monument at all. It looks real!" Having established himself as something of an expert on Lincoln, the sculptor then sounded off with typical vociferation against the announced plans for the Lincoln Memorial, which he regarded, he wrote his friend Felix Frankfurter, "with pain akin to madness.... A modernized twentieth-century interpretation of a Greek temple to stand there forever on the flats... to remind us of that simple great first gift of the West.... Is it possible that Lincoln is to be dehumanized and rolled into the conventional architectural formula so soon!"

A devotee of T.R.'s "strenuous life," Borglum extended himself in manly sports as well as civic affairs. "I do everything," he explained to a newspaperman who had inquired about his nonartistic activities, "boxing, fencing, wrestling, horseback riding.... A man should do everything, turn handsprings, somersaults. The trouble with American life is that it is not vigorous enough." In politics, despite his rather Caesarian temperament, he was a progressive: pro-labor, pro-Teddy Roosevelt, pro-democracy. The entry of the United States into World War I spun him into a flurry of patriotic zeal. Early an aviation fan,

Impressive from a distance, the colossal physiognomies of Mount Rushmore have even greater impact from close up. This photo, taken from atop Washington's head, shows Jefferson's nose and Lincoln's face.
AUTHOR'S COLLECTION

he was convinced that American production of warplanes was seriously deficient, and persuaded Woodrow Wilson to let him come to Washington to investigate the situation. Angry and confused when Wilson appeared to brush aside the accusatory and troublesome report he made after a month of hard work, Borglum sent an open letter to newspapers denouncing the President's negligence. Wilson, meanwhile, who had expected a gadfly and raised a hornet, declared: "I never at any time constituted you an official investigator." Borglum, thoroughly disenchanted but still out to win the war, went back to his big studio and estate in Stamford, Connecticut, where he set up a camp for the entertainment and training of Czechoslovakian volunteers.

When in the summer of 1927 Borglum was ready to begin the work on Mount Rushmore, he was enough of a national figure to arouse much curiosity over what he would attempt there and whether he would accomplish it. The question of whose faces would be "released" from the mountain had already been settled, mostly as a result of Borglum's adamant insistence: Washington, Jefferson, and Lincoln were easy choices, but Theodore Roosevelt aroused argument. He had been a personal friend of Borglum's, which of course raised some suspicion of favoritism; but the sculptor was ready with his rationale. T.R., he said, was an "all-American President" who had made America a world power with the Panama Canal and who with his three great predecessors formed a quartet magnificently representative of the building of the nation.

About one thing there was never any doubt: the sculpture was going to be tremendous. Although Borglum later was annoyed by tourists whose only reaction to the monument was open-mouthed wonder at its size, he fully intended from the beginning that its proportions should be stunning. They should be determined, he said, "by the importance to civilization of the events commemorated"; and he told Senator Norbeck that his mission was "to get the American

people to look at art in a big way and to get away from this petty stuff." The great stone faces would measure sixty feet from hairline to chin; the noses would average twenty feet long; the mouths eighteen feet wide; the eye sockets eleven feet across. On that scale, if the figures of Washington and Lincoln were to be completed full length they would be about 465 feet tall, more than three times the height of the Colossus of Rhodes, one of the Seven Wonders of the ancient world.

The cutting of the granite got off to a prestigious start as a result of Calvin Coolidge having been persuaded, by Norbeck and others, that he ought to spend the summer of 1927 in the Black Hills where mountain trout twenty inches long were easy to catch. (They were easy to catch because a great many of them, carefully bred, were dumped at the right times into the streams where the unsuspecting President fished.) It was not many miles from the summer White House at Custer State Park's Game Lodge to Mount Rushmore, and early in August, having stuffed his trouser legs into cowboy boots and placed a big sombrero unjauntily on his head, Coolidge was conveyed by automobile and gentle horse to the site of the monument.

Borglum was ready. Never a man to forgo pomp for mere practicality, he managed to combine the two by having twenty-one tree stumps blown up in well-timed succession as Coolidge progressed along the road that was being built to the mountain. The President delivered a brief but, for him, eloquent speech, calling Mount Rushmore a national shrine whose "cornerstone... was laid by the hand of the Almighty"; then Borglum went up the mountain and with great panache swung down over its face in a specially designed sling seat attached to a cable and drilled a few initial holes for points on Washington's face. The crowd of nearly two thousand applauded mightily.

One curious result of Coolidge's visit to Mount Rushmore was that he undertook to compose a suitable historical inscription, to be carved into a hugh entablature on the mountain in letters so large and deep that they

23

could be read for three miles. (The arrangement with Coolidge was made part of Public Law 805, passed in 1929, setting up the Mount Rushmore National Memorial Commission to supervise construction of the monument.) Borglum was not willing to settle for an inspirational quotation of some sort: he wanted about five hundred words that would epitomize if not summarize all of American history. The best way to do this, he thought, was to pick out eight or ten pivotal events and write a pithy explanatory statement about each one.

Coolidge, his famous laconicism at stake, labored long and hard on this grave assignment. In the spring of 1932 it was announced that the former President had completed statements for the first two events, namely the Declaration of Independence and the adoption of the Constitution. As given out to eager newspapers by a public relations firm Borglum had hired, the proposed inscriptions read:

"In the year of our Lord 1776 the people declared the eternal right to seek happiness, self-government and the divine duty to defend that right at any sacrifice."

"In 1787 assembled in convention they made a charter of perpetual union for free people of sovereign states establishing a government of limited powers under an independent President, Congress, and Court charged to provide security for all citizens in their enjoyment of liberty, equality, and justice."

Press commentary across the nation soon indicated a widespread feeling that this left something to be desired in eloquence, grandeur, and even grammar—especially for words that were to be carved in granite and might well endure for 500,000 years. Debate along this line, however, quickly gave way to dismay and some snickers when Borglum admitted, under prodding, that he had edited Coolidge's prose considerably without consulting the distinguished author. Coolidge's original text had read:

"The Declaration of Independence—The eternal right to seek happiness through self-government and the divine duty to defend that right at any sacrifice."

"The constitution—charter of perpetual union of free people of sovereign states establishing a government of limited powers—under an independent President, Congress, and Court, charged to provide security for all citizens in their enjoyment of liberty, equality and justice under the law."

While it was doubtful that Borglum had improved these pronouncements, there was no doubt that Calvin Coolidge was extremely irked at his wielding of the blue pencil. "I do not wish to approve the changes...," he informed the sculptor. "In each instance it breaks up the thought I was trying to convey." A mutual acquaintance, Paul Bellamy of Rapid City, reported later that when he was paying his respects to the retired President in Northampton, Massachusetts, Coolidge asked how far it was to the Black Hills and was told it was about two thousand miles. "You know," said Coolidge, "that is just about as close to Mr. Borglum as I want to be." The brouhaha over Borglum's editing of Coolidge put the whole question of the inscribed entablature up in the air,

AUTHOR'S COLLECTION

**HEAP
BIG
HEAP**

and in the end it was abandoned. Most lovers of Mount Rushmore felt that this was just as well.

The carving of Mount Rushmore took fourteen years, although it has been figured that without the numerous interruptions for lack of funds, it could have been done in six and a half. The process was complex, and involved engineering skills as much as those of art. Borglum had been overly optimistic in his estimate of the mountain's solidity: some of the fissures on its side turned out to be deep, and the quality of the rock uneven. Thousands of tons of granite had to be dynamited away before a workable surface was reached. Washington's finished chin, for example, is thirty feet back of the original surface; Jefferson's is about sixty feet; Teddy Roosevelt, waiting (in Borglum's metaphor) to be released from the granite, was found lurking so far back—120 feet—that a great nervousness developed as to whether he was really there at all; for a canyon runs close behind the heads, and the available rock was distinctly finite.

Jefferson's head was begun on the opposite side of Washington's from

A few miles from Mount Rushmore there is a mountain-carving project that, theoretically, ought to please the Indians a good deal more than the famous heads of the four Presidents. If ever completed, it will be a stunningly large equestrian statue of Chief Crazy Horse, the Sioux leader who fought nobly for his people and helped do in Custer at the Little Bighorn.

The planned dimensions of the Crazy Horse monument match the ego of its creator, sculptor-genius (as he describes himself) Korczak Ziolkowski: 563 feet high, 641 feet long, an 87½-foot head for the Chief and a 219-foot head for his pony ("enough space for a five-room house in each of the horse's nostrils," Ziolkowski says).

But tourists who turn off the highway about four miles north of Custer, South Dakota, to drive to Thunderhead Mountain and observe the Crazy Horse carving are likely to be disappointed. First of all, they are

where it is now, but one of Borglum's assistants made a bad mistake in cutting, and there was insufficient depth for correction. The unfinished face was blasted away in 1934 and a new start made at Washington's left shoulder—which, however, had to be drastically recut to make room for Jefferson's chin. Then a long crack was found where the new Jeffersonian nose had been planned, and Borglum had to "reset" the head at a different angle and several feet farther back. "I have no intention," he said, "of leaving a head on that mountain that in the course of five hundred or five thousand years will be without a nose."

It is remarkable that, confronting such problems, Borglum was able to impart to the monument the look of carefully conceived artistic work. He did it by always being ready to rethink the overall composition, again and again departing from his studio model in order to meet the tough exigencies of the granite. Moreover, although the features of the four Presidents, magnified on a scale of a foot to an inch, could be transferred from model to mountain with amazing accuracy by means of an elaborate system of measurement and triangulation, the artist made many subtle changes, as each face neared completion, because of the actual look of the thing. Just as an ordinary sculptor steps back a few yards from a statue to consider its effect, Borglum would often drive several miles to another mountain, climb it, and study his work across the distance with binoculars. Then he would go back, have himself lowered from Rushmore's top in his sling seat, and mark the spots where he wanted a little more rock removed to improve a presidential facial expression.

One of the sculptor's most notable refinements was in the treatment of the eyes. For the two faces first completed, Washington's and Jefferson's, the pupils were represented by granite shafts, about twenty inches long, left attached to the inside of the eyes at the top, so that they stick down like stalactites. These reflect daylight in a way that, in contrast to the dark shadows within the eyes, gives a lifelike look; but Borglum discovered later that having the granite pupils project straight out from the middle of the eyes was even better. Lincoln and Teddy Roosevelt were therefore done that way, to truly startling effect. T.R's famous pince-nez offered another chance for ingenuity, and the artist managed to suggest them so well merely by carving a curved ridge under a part of each eye that many viewers swear they can see the lenses.

Very little of the Mount Rushmore monument was carved with mallet and chisel, new techniques having been devised to suit the gigantic scope of the undertaking. Once a key point had been "located" in the granite by measurement and triangulation—say the end of a nose—Borglum's crew of trained workmen would dynamite away the rock to within a few inches of the final surface. Rough shaping of noses, cheeks, mouths, and other features was done both by dynamiting, and by wedging off layers of granite after honeycombing the appropriate area with holes made by heavy pneumatic drills. Finer shaping was then achieved by "bumping" the granite down to a smooth surface, using a special pneumatic tool equipped with a four-point steel bit.

Borglum, while he did relatively little of the physical work himself, was

charged two dollars per car to get into the grounds. Then, ushered out upon a terrace where a big plaster model of the monument glistens in the sunlight, they hear a spiel explaining how Ziolkowski, "the grandson of a Polish count" (but born in Boston), has been working on the mountain for over a quarter of a century, without state or federal aid; how several million tons of granite have been blasted away already; what the historical significance of the statue will be, etc.

The trouble is that when the tourists lift their eyes to the mountain itself, all they see is a vast expanse of granite that looks as if perhaps it has been subjected to strip mining. Through pay binoculars on the terrace it is possible to make out a few machines and cables on slopes of the mountain, a certain amount of shaping along the top, and a relatively small hole that has been punched through where, allegedly, the space under Crazy Horse's outstretched arm will be. Even with the help of the hole it is very difficult to visualize the finished monument. Many visitors express disbelief that it will ever be completed.

For consolation they can buy refreshments (including buffalo burgers) and souvenirs (including replicas of the Crazy Horse Monument, or rather of the model, in assorted sizes); they can also go on a guided tour of the sprawling fifty-seven-room building that is Ziolkowski's combination home, studio, and museum. There are many wood carvings and pieces in other media to testify that the sixty-eight-year-old Ziolkowski really is a sculptor, and whole walls covered with illustrated articles about him cut from newspapers and magazines. A row of marble heads of famous people lines the walk leading from the parking lot into the main building; all of them have been deprived of their noses by someone equipped with a sledge hammer and, apparently, an intense dislike for Ziolkowski.

What do the Indians think of the Crazy Horse project? Back when Ziolkowski was getting started, he drew encouraging words from an eminent Sioux, Chief Henry Standing Bear: "Please carve us a mountain so the white man will know that the red man had great heroes, too." That was before the days of the American Indian Movement (AIM) and the surge for "red power." "Crazy Horse never let a white man take his picture," observed Lame Deer, a Sioux medicine man and activist, a few years ago. "The whole idea of making a beautiful wild mountain into a statue of him is a pollution of the landscape." Said another, Fools Crow: "This mountain doesn't want the statue to be built. The ghost of Crazy Horse doesn't want it. It will never be finished." —E.M.H.

often on the working face of the mountain, hovering over every detail. An intimidating boss when he was on the job—"If the Old Man said it was going to rain and the sun was shining, I said, 'It sure looks like rain,'" one of his workmen reported—the artist was also found to be irascible and hard to work with by many others interested in seeing Mount Rushmore completed. Senator Norbeck, who was fond of Borglum despite painful altercations, observed that "his unwillingness to cooperate with anyone else is simply astonishing."

This was especially awkward for the creator of a project that sometimes teetered toward bankruptcy and in the long run had to be bailed out by congressional appropriations. A concomitant of this was that in June, 1933, Franklin D. Roosevelt placed Mount Rushmore under the jurisdiction of the National Park Service—a move that seemed possibly ominous, since the Service's determination to keep things natural was legendary, and Mount Rushmore was anything but natural. Nothing much happened for three years, but in 1936 a "resident engineer" was assigned to the project by the government agency. The engineer, an affable and capable man named Julian C. Spotts, quickly set about installing a small cable car to obviate the daily climb up Mount Rushmore's steep slope, and made other improvements such as increasing the efficiency of the compressed-air system that operated the drills. Borglum, who could not stomach anything that remotely resembled supervision, responded by complaining bitterly about what he saw as Spott's bureaucratic administrative arrangements, and soon was conducting his negotiations with the engineer in writing although their offices on the site were almost adjacent.

This was fairly typical. The sculptor was in the habit, when particularly irritated at someone, of sending the begetter of his irritation a vitriolic letter, with carbon copies to congressmen, editors, or others who he thought should know of the fardels under which he labored. This did not win him many friends; yet he had many, for when a more genial humor seized him, Borglum could be notably charming and generous. During the Depression, for instance, he was greatly moved by the destitute state of the Indians on South Dakota's Pine Ridge Reservation, and expended much time and effort gathering large contributions of food and blankets for them. The Sioux made him an honorary chief—Chief Stone Eagle—in gratitude.

Despite Borglum's thorny behavior toward the Park Service's operative, F.D.R. decided to take a detour to Mount Rushmore while on a trip to survey Dust Bowl agricultural distress in August, 1936. The timing was good: Thomas Jefferson's face had finally emerged from the mountain enough to sustain a dedication ceremony. Borglum grew baleful, however, when the presidential party was delayed two hours in arriving at the monument; he growled that afternoon shadows would now fall across Jefferson's face and spoil everything. Nevertheless, when F.D.R. got there the sculptor did one of his quick-change performances, greeting the President with magisterial courtesy. Roosevelt watched with absorption as a few exemplary dynamite blasts blew stone off the monument with a great roar; then little parachutes, released from an airplane and weighted with chips of granite from the mountain, floated down among three thousand spectators while a seventy-foot flag was drawn aside to reveal Jefferson's visage. Genuinely impressed, F.D.R. gave an impromptu and enthusiastic speech, and the event ended with everyone glowing and optimistic.

Mount Rushmore was now better than half finished, for work had begun on Lincoln and Theodore Roosevelt. Borglum had proved that he could do the job if only the money problems could continue to be solved and the trouble caused by his contentiousness could be kept down to some reasonable level. A full account of the vicissitudes of the project in South Dakota and in Washington, where advocates steadily sought more government money for the monument, and of Borglum's bickering with the National Park Service and the Mount Rushmore national commission would be very long and complicated (though such an account has been given in Gilbert C. Fite's excellent book *Mount Rushmore* [1952], which remains by far the most thorough historical study of the whole subject).

Here it is enough to tick off highlights: the dedication of the Lincoln head in September, 1937; Borglum's surprising luck in getting passage of new federal legislation in June, 1938, removing Mount Rushmore from the National Park Service's control and authorizing $300,000 more toward finishing the work; F.D.R.'s decision, a year later, to reinstate control by the Service (since it was now clear that eventually the monument grounds would require careful planning and administration in order to be adequate for the expected crowds of tourists); the dedication of Theodore Roosevelt's head in July, 1939. A visionary scheme of the sculptor to cut an enormous "Hall of Records" in the granite canyon up behind the great heads—to contain permanent records of American history, carved inscriptions, busts of other national heroes, etc., etc.—met with stubborn resistance from the Park Service and came to almost nothing, although Borglum, just as stubborn, did spend some $16,000 blasting a big square hole—the entrance to the Hall—twenty-five yards back into the stone before he was ordered to cease and desist. (It is still there, bleak and empty.)

By the late winter of 1941 work on the great stone faces was substantially finished. Borglum, now nearly seventy-four years old, underwent a prostate operation in Chicago in February. He came through it well, but developed a blood clot and died suddenly on March 6. Lincoln Borglum, who had been his father's chief assistant since 1931, giving up college to do so, carried on the work; and before America turned all its attention to World War II on December 7, the last carving had been done on Mount Rushmore. Had Gutzon Borglum lived, and had more money been available, the figures would have been somewhat more fully realized; but his son judged that they were satisfactorily done.

In the thirty-six years since the monument received its final touches, Mount Rushmore has become one of the most alluring tourist attractions in the country. Though remote from urban centers, it is serviced by excellent highways and surrounded by gorgeous scenery; it also enjoys a splendid climate for most of the spring, summer, and fall. The well-appointed grounds—a modern visitors' center, a viewing terrace, Borglum's studio, a commodious amphitheater for outdoor programs in full view of the monument, a concessions building with a cafeteria and a large shop where souvenirs ranging from the absurd to the acceptable are on sale—are administered by the National Park Service with almost antiseptic efficiency, and the big parking lot is seldom if ever empty. Courteous rangers (including, in the summer months, a few lissome college girls in Smokey-the-Bear hats) answer questions, take part in special programs, and watch the slopes of the mountain to stop violators of the no-climbing rule ("Violators subject to fine of $500 and 6 months in jail"). Over two million people came to Mount Rushmore in 1976, to stare admiringly at the great faces, take countless pictures, wander about, and write in the visitors' register comments like "Inspiring!" "Magnificent!" "Far out!" or "Makes me proud to be an American." (These are salted very occasionally by such remarks as "Waste!")

Borglum was anxious that the monument should not be regarded as "just a damn big thing": that full value should also be accorded its artistic worth and its historical significance. The difficulty of eliciting a balanced reaction was brought home to him one day when he stopped along a road a few miles from Rushmore to chat with a man who was offering telescopic views of the nearly completed sculpture to passing motorists. "What do people say when they look at the mountain?" the artist inquired. The entrepreneur was reluctant, but finally came across: "Most folks want to know how much concrete it took." That gave Borglum a good laugh. "What do you tell them?" he asked. "I tell them I don't rightly know," said the man. "How much *did* it take?"

The Park Service is assiduous, in its brochures and in the recorded "terrace talk" heard continuously over its PA system, to stress the lofty intent and symbolism of the monument over its sheer size (". . . The Memorial serves to remind all Americans of this country's noble achievements of the past and the hope a democratic society offers for the future. . . ."). The fact remains that Mount Rushmore's fantastic proportions and its spectacular mountain setting have been its most impressive aspects: there is simply no other work of sculpture in the world to compare with this American colossus. As for its artistic worth, if it has not evoked much praise from critics it surely must be ranked among Borglum's best works, all of which are in a naturalistic tradition not admired by the aesthetic arbiters of recent times.

This photo of a Sioux "warrior" in full headdress posing before Mount Rushmore suggests a travel publicity stunt, but in fact was taken by a tourist, in 1961, of an Indian named Black Dog who was there to agitate for Indian representation in the South Dakota legislature.
DON VINCENT GRAY

When it comes to judging Mount Rushmore's value as a "shrine of democracy" (the phrase belonged to F.D.R.)—as an emblematic projection of American ideals—there has also been room for argument. The Indian occupation of the memorial in 1970 was a straw in the wind blowing toward far more serious demands for Indian reparations and self-determination, such as the violent confrontation at Wounded Knee in 1973. The occupation served not so much as a criticism of the monument itself as of the history it purports to celebrate. Yet the four famous men whose faces scan the country from Mount Rushmore were all profoundly concerned with justice, which is the heart of the matter. If the society they represent can remember and hold fast to that, then it, as well as their heroic images, may endure as long as even Gutzon Borglum could have dreamed. ☆

THE FIRST FOURTH

John Adams was certain the second of July would be celebrated "by succeeding generations, as the great anniversary Festival." Writing to his wife Abigail on July 3, 1776, the day after the Continental Congress had voted momentously for independence from Great Britain, Adams said of July 2:

"It ought to be commemorated, as the Day of Deliverance by solemn Acts of Devotion to God Almighty. It ought to be solemnized with Pomp and Parade, with Shews, Games, Sports, Guns, Bells, Bonfires and Illuminations from one End of this Continent to the other from this Time forward forever more."

America's independence has indeed always been observed with such festivities, but Adams was wrong about the day. It was the adoption two days later of the Declaration of Independence, the document explaining the reasons for the separation from Great Britain, that Americans chose to celebrate. The Declaration, which was widely distributed throughout the new nation in broadside form, was of course dated July 4, 1776.

One year to that day the very first commemorations were held in some of the major cities of the thirteen states, Philadelphia among them. That city may have been the cradle of liberty, but its citizens were by no means united in the patriot cause (as became all too evident later in 1777 when British troops occupied it). A grand round of parades, banquets, and fireworks was prepared, but Philadelphia's Executive Council, fearing violence, urgently requested all constables and watchmen to be on patrol that evening, and called up two hundred militiamen "to direct in preserving the peace"—and, no doubt, to protect captured Hessian musicians who were to perform.

What especially worried the city fathers was the "illumination" attending the Fourth of July observance. At sunset, patriots planned to light candles and lanterns inside and outside their homes. Tory houses would be conspicuous by their darkness. With that in mind, the Executive Council recommended "moderation & forbearance towards persons who might not illuminate."

How did that first Fourth go? One journal, *Dunlap's Penn Packet*, recorded the event:

"Last Friday the 4th of July, being the anniversary of the Independence of the United States of America, was celebrated in this City with demonstrations of joy and festivity. About noon all the armed ships and gallies in the river were drawn up before the City, dressed in the gayest manner, with the colours of the United States and streamers displayed. At one o'clock, the yards being properly manned, they began the celebration of the day by a discharge of thirteen cannon from each of the ships, and one from each of the thirteen gallies, in honor of the thirteen United States.

"In the afternoon an elegant dinner was prepared for Congress, to which were invited the President and Supreme Executive Council, and Speaker of the Assembly of this State, the general officers and colonels of the army, and strangers of eminence, and the Members of the Several Continental Boards in Town. The Hessian band of music, taken in Trenton the 26th of December last, attended and heightened the festivity with some fine performances suited to the joyous occasion, while a corps of British deserters, taken into the service of the continent by the State of Georgia, being drawn up before the door, filled up the intervals with *Feux De Joie*. After dinner a number of toasts were drank, all breathing independence, and a generous love of liberty, and commemorating the memories of those brave and worthy patriots who gallantly exposed their lives, and fell gloriously in defence of freedom and the righteous cause of their country.

"Each toast was followed by a discharge of artillery and small arms, and a suitable piece of music by the Hessian Band.

"The glorious fourth of July was reiterated three times, accompanied with triple discharges of cannon and small arms, and loud huzzas that resounded from street to street through the city. Towards evening several troops of horse, a corps of artillery, and a brigade of North Carolina forces, which was in town on its way to join the Grand Army, were drawn up in Second Street, and reviewed by Congress and the General Officers. The evening was closed with the ringing of bells, and at night there was a grand exhibition of fireworks (which began and concluded with thirteen rockets) on the Commons, and the City was beautifully illuminated. Everything was conducted with the greatest order and decorum, and the face of joy and gladness was universal.

"Thus may the Fourth of July, that glorious and ever memorable day, be celebrated through America, by the Sons of Freedom, from age to age till time shall be no more. Amen, and Amen."

A fourth July scene about the year 1795 as then sketched from a position on the south line of Chesnut St — showing that then the whole area was a grass commons, from Chesnut to Spruce St — & from 6th St westward.

west side of Prison.

Papist Chapel

Something of the "Pomp and Parade" that John Adams suggested would be appropriate for celebrating America's independence is depicted in the water color above by John Fanning Watson. The artist presumably witnessed this "fourth [of] July scene about the year 1795" while working as a teen-age countinghouse clerk in Philadelphia. Watson later became a leading financier and a chronicler of the city's history. This painting is one of several made from memory as a guide for the lithographer who illustrated Watson's classic Annals of Philadelphia, which was published in 1830.

LIBRARY COMPANY OF PHILADELPHIA

Ordeal at Vella Lavella

by Walter Lord

The U.S.S. *Helena* (above) on fire

Six thousand miles southwest of San Francisco lie the Solomon Islands, scene of perhaps the bitterest fighting ever waged by Americans at war. Here, in 1942–43, the United States and its allies battled the empire of Japan for mastery of the South Pacific.

Geographically, the Solomons are a majestic chain stretching from Buka and Bougainville, just below the equator, to San Cristobal six hundred miles to the southeast. For most of this distance the chain splits into two parallel lines of islands separated by a corridor of water known as "The Slot." Strategically, the Solomons are a spear pointing directly at the line of communication between Australia and the United States.

Both sides recognized this, but the Japanese got there first. Continuing the relentless advance that had carried them from Pearl Harbor to the approaches of Australia, the emperor's forces began moving into the northern Solomons toward the end of March, 1942. The handful of defenders could do nothing about it. Their antique weapons were no match for the conquerors of Singapore.

Sensing disaster, most of the European settlers—several hundred planters, traders, and officials—fled south, but here and there a few stayed behind to weather the invasion. Some were missionaries, held by the call of God; a few were volunteers answering the more terrestrial orders of an Australian naval officer, Commander Eric Feldt. These were called Coastwatchers.

Aided by friendly natives and equipped with "teleradios"—remarkably durable sets that would transmit by either voice or telegraph key—the Coastwatchers lived by their wits behind the Japanese lines, sending a steady flow of priceless information. Their mission was to observe, not fight; and to remind them, Feldt called his operation "Ferdinand" after the peaceful bull of fiction.

One such observer was Henry Josselyn on the island of Vella Lavella in the central Solomons. A small, spry Englishman, Josselyn had served in the local colonial government before the war. Unlike most of the Coastwatchers, he was not already at his post when the Japanese came. He was slipped in by submarine in October, 1942, after the U.S. Marines had landed on Guadalcanal to set the stage for a great counteroffensive.

During the following months Josselyn organized a network of native scouts, radioed regular reports on Japanese plane and ship movements, rescued thirty-one downed American flyers, and kept an eye on the enemy outposts on Vella Lavella. In July, 1943, he was based on a mountain that directly overlooked the main Japanese camp. At this time he was assisted by a young Australian, Robert Firth.

But they were not the only men operating secretly on Vella Lavella. Also on hand was the Reverend A.W.E. Silvester, a Methodist missionary from New Zealand who had remained on the island, eluding Japanese patrols with the assistance of his flock. "Wattie" Silvester was a dedicated man of the cloth, but more than once he found himself quietly helping Josselyn and Firth.

In the early days of July, as the Allied advance brought the fighting closer, these three men suddenly faced a challenge unparalleled even in the dangerous and sometimes bizarre world of the Coastwatchers. It all began with one of those slam-bang naval actions in The Slot that were so much a part of the war in the Solomons. . . . W.L.

PRECEDING PAGE: NAVY DEPARTMENT PHOTO, NATIONAL ARCHIVES

Later, after it was all over, Lieutenant Commander John L. Chew decided that his big mistake was shaving that day. Chew was assistant gunnery officer on the light cruiser *Helena* and a typically superstitious sailor. He always wore the same pair of old brown shoes and flashproof coveralls. (The coveralls, in fact, were so important he wouldn't let them be washed.) He always carried his lucky hunting knife on his belt, his lucky four-leaf clover in his wallet, his lucky silver dollar in his pocket. And he never, never shaved before going into battle.

This time it had seemed perfectly safe to spruce up a little. After a hard night's work supporting the landings on New Georgia, the *Helena* was steaming south, away from the action, presumably for a few days of rest.

Then late in the afternoon of July 5 came word that the "Tokyo Express" was on the move again. Ten destroyers were heading down The Slot, bringing reinforcements for Major General Noboru Sasaki's hard-pressed defenders at Munda, the main Japanese stronghold on New Georgia. The *Helena*, along with the rest of Rear Admiral Walden L. Ainsworth's force of cruisers and destroyers, was ordered to turn around immediately and intercept. For Jack Chew the word came too late—he had already shaved.

By 1:30 A.M. on the sixth the force was off the mouth of Kula Gulf, racing up The Slot at 25 knots. Clouds hid the moon, but the towering volcanic cone of Kolombangara Island loomed to port. At 1:36 the radarman made contact—seven to nine ships coming out of Kula Gulf, hugging the Kolombangara shore.

Japanese lookouts soon sighted the Americans, too, and when Ainsworth's force opened fire at 1:57, the enemy destroyers had a nice aiming point for their "long lance" torpedoes.

At 2:04 a roar split the night, and the *Helena* gave a sickening lurch. One of the torpedoes had found its mark, completely tearing off the ship's bow. Thirty seconds later a second torpedo hit . . . then a third. The *Helena* sagged, back broken amidships. All power was gone; guns were silent; communications cut; lights out, except for a few dim emergency bulbs.

Jack Chew, in charge of the Combat Information Center, checked the bridge for instructions. Captain Charles P. Cecil's orders were no surprise—abandon ship. The word spread, and men poured onto the slanting decks. Chew and Lieutenant Commander Warren Boles, the *Helena*'s gunnery officer, struggled to get the life rafts off the forecastle into the water. Farther aft, Major Bernard T. Kelly, commanding the ship's Marine detachment, checked the main deck forward to make sure no one was left behind, then climbed down a cargo net into the sea. Near the stern, Ensign George Bausewine, a young assistant damage control officer, carefully removed his shoes and slipped into the water.

Swimming clear, they all turned for a last look at the *Helena*. The bow and stern rose high in the air to form a V. Then with a rumble she slid straight down, disappearing at

COPYRIGHT © 1977 BY WALTER LORD

In this Marine Corps painting, a B-24 makes a low run to drop rubber rafts to survivors of the sunken U.S.S. Helena. *The sailors and Marines in the water are clinging desperately to pieces of floating wreckage from their torpedoed ship. In 1918, George Harding, who painted this water color, had been a combat artist with the American Expeditionary Forces in Europe. Although he was close to sixty when World War II broke out, Harding again went into uniform—this time as a Marine captain—to record historic scenes of Americans at war.*

U.S. MARINE CORPS ART COLLECTION

about 2:30 A.M. Watching her go, Major Kelly felt as if his home had burned to the ground.

For the next hour hundreds of men milled around in the water, hoping that some ship might pick them up. The lucky ones found rafts; the rest gathered in clusters where they might be more easily seen. Chew and Boles collected a group of about seventy-five around a Jacob's ladder that came floating by.

Sometime before dawn they heard ships approaching, and soon Major Kelly made out the number *449* on the bow of a destroyer. That meant the *Nicholas,* one of Ainsworth's force. The Admiral had detached her with the destroyer *Radford* to look for survivors, once he realized the *Helena* was missing. The rest of the task force was now high-tailing it back to Tulagi, convinced they had wiped out most of the Japanese fleet. Actually, they had sunk only one destroyer, with another driven on a reef through bad navigation.

The *Nicholas* and the *Radford* lowered nets and boats and began taking survivors aboard. For many, like Ensign Bausewine, rescue seemed only seconds off. He was floating on his back right next to one of the destroyers, awaiting his turn to climb aboard. Then, without warning, she suddenly got under way at high speed and began firing her guns. Another Japanese destroyer had been sighted coming out of Kula Gulf. The fight was on again.

Dawn was now breaking, and with Japanese planes controlling these skies, there was no chance for the destroyers to come back again. Amazingly, in the short time they had been at the scene, they had managed to pick up 745 survivors; their boats—left behind as they steamed off—took another hundred to a safe spot on the New Georgia coast.

The rest of the *Helena* survivors, including Jack Chew's group, remained treading water in The Slot. With daylight they found a curious rallying point. The *Helena*'s bow, severed from the ship by the first torpedo, was still afloat. Standing vertically about twenty feet out of the water, it soon became a popular refuge. Chew and many of the others paddled over, feeling it should be the first thing spotted by any friendly planes that came looking for them. And so it proved. About 10 A.M. a B-24 appeared, circled, and dropped three rubber rafts. One failed to open, but Chew's group managed to inflate the other two. Unfortunately each could hold only four men. Chew put in his most

The Solomons, that scattering of islands so crucial to the safety of Australia, are shown on the large map at left, with Vella Lavella pictured in detail beside it. Above is a view of Vella Lavella's beachfront, showing the jungle growth close to the waterline that provided cover for the exhausted Helena *survivors who were washed ashore.*

seriously injured, and the group continued waiting.

Soon more planes arrived—but this time they were Zeros. Watching them approach, Major Kelly recalled the recent Bismarck Sea affair, when Allied aircraft strafed the Japanese life rafts after sinking their transports. This was no gentleman's war, and he steeled himself for the worst.

But the Zeros didn't shoot. The nearest pilot simply pulled back his canopy and looked at them closely. Circling, the planes made a second run, and again held their fire. As they circled for a third run, they got off a few short bursts, and Kelly felt sure that this would be it: As they roared by, practically touching the water, the lead pilot grinned, waved, waggled his wings . . . and then they were gone. The relieved but puzzled survivors figured they were so coated with fuel oil that the flyers couldn't tell whether they were American or Japanese.

But it was a close call. It drove home to Chew that these were indeed enemy waters, and the bow was far more likely to attract Japanese than American planes. He decided his group, now down to about fifty, should clear out as soon as possible. Kolombangara lay only eight or nine miles to the south. If they used the rafts to get there, maybe they could then work their way to the U.S. lines on New Georgia.

They shoved off around 11 A.M., with the two rafts tied loosely together and the men divided evenly between them. The injured continued to ride as passengers, while two or three hands straddled the rims and paddled; everyone else remained in the water, clinging to the sides, kicking and pushing the craft along.

All that day they inched toward Kolombangara, but it was hard, exhausting work. Chew tried to ease the strain by developing a system of rotation. Every so often one of the swimmers would take a turn in the raft itself, along with the injured. But there was room for only one or two at a time, and as things worked out, a man could expect only ten minutes of rest every two hours.

Nightfall, and Kolombangara seemed as far away as ever. One of the injured men died, and all were badly off. It had now been eight hours since they had left the dubious refuge of the *Helena*'s bow. They were bone-tired, hungry, and utterly discouraged. Under a tropical sky blazing with stars that seemed far nearer than the island they were trying to reach, Chew led them all in the Lord's Prayer.

As the night wore on, the yearning for sleep grew

overwhelming. No matter how hard they fought it, some succumbed, loosened their grip, and were gone for good. Major Kelly knew the danger, and tried desperately to stay awake. Once he nodded, found himself floating away from the group, and barely made it back. Next time, he stayed asleep, and when a mouthful of salt water woke him up, it was almost dawn and he was alone in the sea.

He started swimming north, and if he needed any stimulus, it was provided by two fish, about three or four feet long, that showed great interest in his bare feet. He splashed, shouted, kicked, and they departed. He continued swimming and finally lucked into one of Chew's two rafts. They had become separated, and this was not Kelly's original one, but no sight was ever more welcome.

By now it was clear to the men on both rafts—and also to the *Helena* survivors clinging to other rafts and bits of wreckage—that they would never get to Kolombangara. Both wind and current were carrying them steadily northwest. Their best hope lay in Vella Lavella, the next island up The Slot.

On Chew's raft someone suggested rigging their shirts as a sail. Two paddles were lashed together to form a crosstree, and the shirts were then stretched between them. Warren Boles was the guiding light. He was from Marblehead, Massachusetts, and had known how to sail before he could ride a bike.

The men's spirits rose, and they perked up even more when a crate of potatoes floated near. For most it was their first food since leaving the *Helena*. But at sundown they were still a long way from Vella Lavella, and it was clear they would be spending another night in the water. Their hearts again sank.

It was as bad as they feared. Kelly's raft lost ten during the night—mostly men who quietly slipped off while the rest were blindly kicking away. By now the men were so exhausted, hallucinations were common. George Bausewine, dozing on the edge of one of the *Helena*'s doughnut rafts, awoke going under the water to get to a bunk he felt sure was there. A groggy, waterlogged Ensign David Chennault kept asking Bausewine for a cigarette.

At daylight on the eighth, discipline collapsed completely on Chew's raft. The men wouldn't rotate any longer. Those resting simply refused to get back in the water, and Chew was too weak to make them do it. Seeing he had lost control, he decided to swim for it. Vella Lavella looked pretty close now; once ashore, maybe he could get some native help.

Warren Boles and two other men joined him, and around 7 A.M. the four pushed off. Two hours ... three hours ... six hours passed. Clearly Vella Lavella was much farther off than it looked. Exhausted, they drifted apart and lost sight of each other. By mid-afternoon Chew was only half-awake. Sometimes he found himself swimming in the wrong direction; other times he went deep under water for no logical reason. He kept thinking he was going to meet a man who would take him to a cocktail party at "the Residency"—whatever that was.

Boles, the best swimmer, seemed more aware of things. Spotting a stretch of beach he liked, he methodically made for it. Stumbling ashore, he found a coconut in the sand, cracked it open for a drink. Then he crawled under a bush a few yards inland and went to sleep.

By 4 P.M. Chew was just about all-in, when he sighted two natives paddling a canoe toward him. They eased alongside and asked, "You American?" "You betcha!" he replied, and they rolled him into the canoe. One of the natives looked so venerable, Chew thought of him as Moses. Reaching shore, they explained they would hide him, and asked if he could walk. Certainly, Chew replied, and collapsed in his tracks.

For ten miles along the beach a remarkable scene began to unfold. Native canoes darted out, plucking men from the water. At other points, rafts and individual swimmers rolled in with the surf. Here and there dazed men wandered about, trying to get their bearings. Coxswain Chesleigh Grunstad felt overwhelmingly content. He had no idea where he was, but even if he had been told the truth—that Vella Lavella was a Japanese-held island sixty miles from the nearest American outpost—at this moment he wouldn't have cared. He was on dry land at last.

Looking down the beach, he could see others coming ashore. Then one man was washed up almost at his feet. He was wearing a red money belt, and it reminded Grunstad of his own money, a roll of two-dollar bills fastened to his dog tags. He loosened the roll and began drying the bills. The other man began doing the same—only his bills were all twenties.

Major Kelly stuck to his raft all the way in. Finally ashore, he had his party hide it under some trees. They were just in time. Minutes later a flight of Japanese dive bombers roared by, only four hundred feet overhead. Kelly next sent a man along the beach in each direction to scout out the situation. The man who went southward returned in a few minutes with a 25-pound can of coffee—at last they were beginning to get some breaks. The other man returned with a *Helena* sailor and a dignified, middle-aged native who introduced himself as Aaron, "a good Christian and a good Methodist." He quickly produced some coconuts, then disappeared to get help.

It was a quiet day at Toupalando, the little village high in the interior of Vella Lavella where the Coastwatcher Henry Josselyn had recently moved his camp. Josselyn had now been on the island more than eight months, reporting Japanese ship and plane movements, rescuing downed airmen, keeping an eye on Iringila, the main Japanese strong point in the area.

So far he had easily dodged the enemy patrols, but they were increasing in number, and when one party landed only three hundred yards from his supply depot at Kila Kila, he had shifted his radio deeper into the interior. This eased the pressure a little, and today he had gone off on some errand, leaving his assistant, Sublieutenant Robert Firth, in charge of the station. A former accountant and ship's purser, Firth was a small, cheerful Australian who quickly adapted himself to coastwatching life.

At the moment, it was not an especially taxing assignment—just a lazy, tropical afternoon. From time to time

The picture, near right, of Reverend A.W.E. Silvester is owned by Captain Warren C. Boles, who at the time of our story was the Helena's *gunnery officer. Captain Boles, now retired, reports that he and "Wattie" corresponded for some years after 1943, and that Silvester sent him the picture. Henry Josselyn, far right, provided the photograph of himself, a tidy, proper picture obviously not taken while he was on Vella Lavella, but roughly at the same time.*

Firth raised his binoculars and checked the Japanese post at Iringila, but nothing unusual was going on. Suddenly the torpor was broken by a native scout hurrying up the path to the camp. Rushing up to Firth, he breathlessly reported "plenty Americans" coming ashore along the east coast. To prove it, he produced a set of U.S. Navy dog tags.

Bobby Firth needed better proof than that. Like most Allied fighting men, he attributed almost limitless guile to the Japanese. He feared this might be just one more of their tricks: a clever charade staged to make the Coastwatchers reveal themselves. He quickly radioed KEN, the base station on Guadalcanal, supplied the name and serial number on the tags, and asked them to check it out.

In an hour KEN was back. The dog tags belonged to a machinist's mate, third class, assigned to the *Helena*, sunk in Kula Gulf on the sixth. Now convinced, Firth sent for Josselyn, who agreed that it looked like "something big." As yet there was no hint as to how many *Helena* survivors were involved, but they seemed to be concentrating in two main groups along the coast—one in the Paraso Bay area, the other twelve miles east near Lambu Lambu village. The Japanese had outposts near both places, and fast work was needed to clear the castaways from the beaches before enemy patrols began picking them up.

A runner dashed off to alert Bamboo, the native chief in the area where the survivors were landing. He was to send out canoes to pick up any men still in the water, plant a string of sentries to watch for Japanese patrols, and stand by to help with food and housing.

Another messenger hurried to the Reverend A.W.E. Silvester, the coastwatching missionary, who was currently at Maravari on the southeast coast. He would take charge of the eastern group of survivors landing near Lambu Lambu. Josselyn himself would take on the western group, at Paraso Bay and Java. Firth would stay at Toupalando—and later at a camp still deeper in the interior—handling the teleradio traffic with KEN. They would all keep in touch through two walkie-talkies and a somewhat larger set used by Josselyn; and to help Firth out they had the fortuitous services of a "guest"—Lieutenant Eli Ciunguin, a P-38 pilot awaiting evacuation.

Everything set, Josselyn headed for the village of Java, where the first survivors had been sighted. Time was so important that he traveled all night to get there.

Ensign Bausewine's group—rescued from their doughnut raft by native canoes—spent the night in leaf huts on the beach near Java. Supper was a hodgepodge of papaya, coconuts, taro, and fish stew. Normally indigestible to Americans, perhaps, but after three days of nothing to eat, nobody complained. It was food.

Shortly after dawn the next morning, July 9, they were awakened by their hosts. Using a mixture of pidgin English and sign language, the natives explained that everyone must leave the beach area. Then, as the group sleepily formed up in the early daylight, out of the jungle appeared a slim white man, hair almost down to his shoulders. It was Henry Josselyn.

Asking for the senior officer present, Josselyn took Bausewine aside and explained how urgent it was to move inland at once. The coast was alive with Japanese patrols and barge traffic. The men were still weak from their three days on the raft, but there was no time for rest. They hobbled inland, camping later in the day, deep in the jungle, where giant trees hid them even from snooping planes.

Twelve miles down the coast a native named Mickey organized the rescue of the other group of survivors at Lambu Lambu Cove. When Ensign Don Bechtel came ashore on the evening of the eighth, one native undressed him, another fed him, a third led him to a clearing where he could rest. More survivors were collected; then, with

37

In contemporary photographs, with the ranks they held at the time of their ordeal on Vella Lavella, are (left column, top to bottom) Lieutenant Commander Warren C. Boles, gunnery officer of the Helena; *Rear Admiral Walden L. Ainsworth, in command of the task group that fought at Kula Gulf; Major Bernard T. Kelly, commander of the* Helena's *Marine detachment; (right column, top) Captain Francis X. McInerney, who was in overall charge of the rescue operation, and (at right, directly above) Lieutenant Commander John L. Chew, the* Helena's *assistant gunnery officer.*

Mickey leading, the group started inland. Those who couldn't walk, like Commander Chew, were carried on litters of poles and copra bags.

Mickey led them first through a jungle swamp, where the men sank up to their knees; then along a hard, rocky trail that climbed into the hills. Finally, after two and a half miles, they came to a clearing with a wooden shanty. To Jack Chew it looked like a typical summer vacation shack on the Chesapeake Bay. It was the house of a Chinese trader named Sam Chung, who was using the building as a hideout in the hills for himself and his family. Sam tactfully moved out, and the place became an impromptu camp for the *Helena* survivors brought up by Mickey. When Chew arrived, Machinist's Mate, First Class, Lloyd George Miller and several others were already there.

Inside, Chew found a few pieces of crude furniture, a shotgun with one shell, a pair of white shorts, and a pair of sneakers. With his own dungarees split and chafing his skin, he tried on the shorts. Miraculously, they fit. Then he tried on the sneakers. Even more miraculously, they fit too.

During the evening more survivors turned up, and then the Reverend Silvester arrived, looking anything but clerical in a short-sleeved shirt and old khaki shorts. A native walked beside him with the walkie-talkie. Searching out Chew, the senior officer, Silvester explained he had "access to a radio" and would have the American headquarters notified.

Next day, the ninth, a few more survivors trickled in. Last to arrive was Warren Boles, who had spent the night on the deserted beach where he landed. Looking around in the morning, he encountered a giant native ("he looked about ten feet tall") armed with a huge machete. Boles had only a six-inch knife, so he did the diplomatic thing. He threw his own knife to the ground and gestured friendship. The native understood no English, but he knew exactly what to do. He led Boles to Sam Chung's house, and with his arrival the group reached a grand total of 104 men.

This was no longer a small band of castaways; this was a whole village—a village deep in enemy territory. To survive, Commander Chew realized they must have rules, assignments, lines of authority, and all the trappings of an organized community. As senior officer, Chew automatically became the "mayor," and it's hard to imagine a better one. A thoroughly professional career officer, he nevertheless had an informal touch that came in handy in these strange surroundings. In the Annapolis world of "black shoe" and "brown shoe" officers, he belonged not only figuratively but literally among the latter, more relaxed group. On the *Helena* his lucky brown shoes had been a trademark.

His "chief of police" was, of course, Major Kelly. He would be in charge of defense, sanitation, and the maintenance of law and order. As a force, Kelly had five of his own Marines plus a number of petty officers and natives.

Weapons were a more difficult problem. At the start the survivors had only a .38 revolver and a .45 automatic. Then Chew discovered the shotgun in Sam Chung's house, and Josselyn sent over seven very assorted rifles, including a Japanese model with exactly three bullets. Two men were assigned to each weapon—if one was hit, the other was to save the gun. The force inevitably became known as "Kelly's Irregulars."

With the Irregulars in the field, Kelly turned his attention to sanitation. Knowing that digging a latrine is not a sailor's idea of fun, he set an example by helping dig it himself. This was no easy task, for their only implement was a steel helmet, unaccountably worn by the ship's barber during the entire three days he was in the water.

They also needed better sleeping quarters. So far, the men were packed in Sam's shack and a curious outbuilding that rather resembled a hen house. The Reverend Silvester said he thought he could remedy this problem, and a team of his mission boys appeared the first morning. Cutting poles and vines from the jungle, they quickly lashed together a framework, then covered the sides with palm leaves, and thatched a roof with grass. By the evening of the tenth they had finished a shed some forty or fifty feet long. To dedicate it, the Reverend Silvester held a service, with survivors and natives joining together in "Onward Christian Soldiers."

Food posed another problem. The natives were short on supplies themselves, and the addition of scores of *Helena* survivors proved a serious drain. Once again the Reverend Silvester came to the rescue. He organized native foraging parties that systematically combed the area. Soon the camp was getting a steady flow of potatoes, tapioca, yams, pau pau, taro root, and bananas. When ripe, the fruit was given to the injured. Everything else was dumped into a huge copper pot, also provided by Silvester's natives. It reminded Jack Chew, a little uncomfortably, of the pots he had seen in cartoons of cannibals cooking missionaries.

The pot was kept boiling by two experienced cooks—Seaman First Class J. L. Johnson and Marine Bert Adam, a massive bartender from Bourbon Street in New Orleans. Twice a day they ladled out a watery stew, laced with a few chunks of Spam scavenged from the beach. The men never ceased to marvel at the results. Sometimes it was rich purple, next time pink, then almost white, and again almost black. There were no complaints, although Coxswain Ted Blahnik later confessed that he tried to dodge the fish eyes.

On medicine, too, the Reverend Silvester proved invaluable. Pharmacist's Mate Red Layton did a superb job with the injured, now bedded down in Sam's shack, but his task was made easier by the sulfa drugs and painkillers that came from the mission stores.

Every evening Silvester dropped by to chat with Jack Chew—not just about the problems of the day, but about life in general. Gradually a close bond developed between them. Bern Kelly and the others felt it too, and they all agreed that this devoted man who did so much for them deserved far more than to be a mere "Reverend." He should at least be a bishop, and so they made him one, unofficially. From this time on, they always called him "Bish."

By July 12 life in "Mayor" Chew's community almost bordered on the routine. In the morning the men got up with the sun—about six o'clock. Washing up without soap was somewhat futile, but they learned that a lime peel was excellent for cleaning teeth.

Breakfast (stew, of course) came around ten, when Chief Cook Johnson would ceremoniously announce, "Chow is ready." Finishing, the men washed the coconut shells that served as plates, and then took two laps around the camp for exercise. Next came cleanup. Nearly everyone had some specific assignment; the most sought-after duty was the canteen detail because it meant an opportunity to bathe in the crystal-clear stream at the bottom of the hill.

Lunch (more stew) came at two o'clock, and that was the last meal of the day. The rest of the afternoon most of the men relaxed, gradually regaining their strength, until evening prayers around five thirty. Not quite knowing how this mixed and involuntary congregation would react, Chew passed the word that no matter how they felt, he expected the men to show proper respect during the Reverend Silvester's service.

He need not have worried. Perilous hardship had brought most of the men closer to God than they had ever been before. Survivors and natives joined together in singing the hymns, especially "Rock of Ages." The natives sang in their language, the *Helena*'s crew in theirs, but the effect was strangely unifying. The common melody seemed to mean a common bond that many of the men found enormously reassuring. It was not unusual to see them in tears as the service ended.

And so the days passed, one pretty much like another—except for the big feast. This took place after a party of natives butchered one of the stray cattle that roamed the island. Lugging the beef back to the camp, the natives were held up by Japanese patrols, and by the time they reached Sam's place, the meat was ripe indeed. Chew consulted Chief Cook Johnson; they reluctantly agreed that it was hopelessly spoiled, and they had it buried. But this was more than Machinist's Mate, Second Class, R. G. Atkinson could stand. He was the oldest member of the *Helena*'s crew, and among other things in life, had been in the Klondike gold rush. He told Chew that in the Yukon no one would throw away beef like that. He knew how to salvage it and would like to try his skill.

The meat was hastily disinterred, and Atkinson went to work. No one ever knew what he really did. Obtaining an iron pot from the natives, he boiled it for three days, occasionally tossing in bits of fruit and herbs he found growing in the jungle. Finally he announced that his treat was ready, and to the astonishment of the other 103 men, it turned out to be delicious.

Despite Atkinson's genius—and the continuing efforts of the more orthodox cooks—food was always short, and always on everyone's mind. The men no longer talked about the girls in Sydney—it was the steaks back home. So it was not too surprising when Major Kelly stormed up to Chew one day, reporting that someone had stolen one of the few cans of Spam salvaged from the rafts. "If I find out who it is, will you sentence him to death?"

Chew said he thought this was a little drastic. The thief was probably some poor devil, so hungry he really didn't

A captured enemy Zero pilot, obviously still terrified, is taken from Vella Lavella along with the rescued American servicemen.
WILLIAM SHROUT. *Life* MAGAZINE © TIME INC.

know what he was doing. Kelly was adamant, and the "Mayor" was caught between approving what he felt was a Draconian measure, or undermining his "Chief of Police." To his enormous relief, the culprit was never caught.

A graver crisis arose the day a four-man Japanese patrol came too close to the camp. The native scouts intercepted, and in the skirmish that followed, three of the enemy were killed. The fourth was taken alive, posing a serious dilemma. With his men hiding out deep in Japanese territory, and the enemy now on their heels, Chew felt it was too dangerous to have a prisoner on their hands, yet they certainly couldn't turn him loose. In the end he reluctantly ordered the Japanese executed—technically, perhaps, against the rules of the Geneva Convention, but surely that body never contemplated a situation like this. Nevertheless it was a hard decision, and it comforted Chew to know that the Reverend Silvester understood and agreed.

The next Japanese thrust was no four-man affair. Twenty well-armed troops landed from a barge in Lambu Lambu Cove and started up the trail toward Sam's house. Warned by their native scouts, the Irregulars deployed to meet the threat, while the rest of Chew's group prepared to move deeper into the interior.

Major Kelly hoped to ambush the Japanese as they climbed single file up the trail. He selected a spot that gave him both good observation and cover for his own men. The Irregulars moved into position with their grab bag of weapons and waited. Soon they heard the Japanese coming, hobnailed boots clanging against the rocks, their voices casual and quite audible in the distance. Kelly wondered how they got their reputation as stealthy jungle fighters.

Still, they were plenty dangerous, and the outnumbered, outgunned Irregulars steeled themselves for a last-ditch fight. Then, just as the head of the enemy column came into view, several blue Corsair fighters streaked by overhead and began firing at the Japanese barge on the coast. Black smoke boiled up, and the patrol, voices babbling in excitement, hurried back to the beach.

Kelly never knew what triggered the attack—probably the fighters just happened by and saw the barge—but he did know that Corsairs were generally land-based. This must mean that the U.S. now had a field within fighter range of Vella Lavella.

Twelve miles up the coast at Paraso Bay—but in touch by radio—Henry Josselyn wasn't thinking about these small triumphs; he was thinking about all the other Japanese on Vella Lavella. Some three to four hundred enemy troops were now on the island, and the number was growing. There were new outposts at Kundurumbangara Point and Baka Baka, both near Chew's camp, and another at Marisi, about three miles west of Ensign Bausewine's group at Paraso.

There was no time to lose, if the men were to be saved. COMSOPAC (as Admiral William Halsey's headquarters was called) said they could provide a couple of destroyer-transports, so the problem boiled down to the mechanics of evacuation. A total of 165 *Helena* survivors were involved—104 with Chew, 50 with Bausewine, and another 11 a few miles to the northwest with Chief Warrant Officer William Dupay. Even after adding Dupay's men to Bausewine's group, it was impossible to concentrate everybody in one place, so Josselyn planned two separate evacuations. He was already at Paraso Bay with Bausewine; so he would send this group off first. Then he would go down to Lambu Lambu and do the same for Chew's group.

July 12, and Bausewine's party received a surprise addition—a captured Zero pilot, brought in by native scouts. Here, too, arose the agonizing question of what to do with the prisoner. The general consensus was to kill him, but as Bausewine later recalled, "Nobody would go through with it; so he lived." Happily, he seemed cowed and thoroughly docile, but to be on the safe side his hands were bound and he was kept blindfolded whenever the group moved. A final and far more welcome newcomer was Lieutenant Ciunguin, the downed P-38 pilot who had been helping Firth with the radio traffic.

By nightfall on the twelfth all were assembled on the beach, waiting for the pickup at 2 A.M., but the Japanese Navy didn't cooperate. The Tokyo Express came barreling down The Slot that night with twelve hundred more reinforcements for Kolombangara. Admiral Ainsworth rushed to intercept them, and the rescue operation was postponed, first to the thirteenth, then to the fourteenth. But now it fell too close to the fifteenth, when Josselyn had planned to send Chew's group off. In the end he proposed to do the whole job on the night of the fifteenth: the ships would first pick up Bausewine's party at Paraso Bay, then steam down the coast and get Chew's group at Lambu Lambu.

COMSOPAC approved, and two tense days of waiting followed. Josselyn knew the Japanese were getting close to Chew, and his own group seemed to be living on borrowed time. He moved the camp every night. He shifted the teleradio after every message. He grew nervous, irritable, smoked incessantly. Bausewine's men gladly smoked his butts, for they had the jitters too. Some jungle bird had a call just like the *Helena* general quarters alarm, and the men jumped every time it sounded off.

On the evening of the fifteenth, the party once again went to the beach. Most of them still had on the shreds of oil-soaked dungarees they had been wearing when they landed, but Bill Dupay was resplendent in the Japanese pilot's uniform. The pilot, blindfolded and hands still tied behind his back, was guided along in his drawers—the fortunes of war.

Twelve miles down the coast, Jack Chew's group was on the move too. With the strongest serving as stretcher-bearers for the sick and wounded, they left the camp at 3 P.M.—a time nicely calculated to get them to Lambu Lambu Cove just before dark. They were in no shape to travel at night, and the coastal plain was too exposed to wait there in broad daylight. Now added to the party were sixteen of the local Chinese—mostly Sam Chung and his relatives.

Kelly's Irregulars screened the movement, taking position between the line of march and the nearest Japanese outpost. Behind them the evacuees plodded along, reaching the coast at dusk, just as planned. The spot selected for the rendezvous was not on the open sea, but at a former trading post dock a mile or so up the Lambu Lambu River. This was a broad estuary with several tricky turns, and Chew assigned Warren Boles, the old Marblehead sailor, to go out in a native canoe and pilot the rescuers in.

It was a far cry from cruising the New England coast. The canoe was paddled by a single native who couldn't speak English and didn't understand any instructions. There was a moon, but the shadows of the jungle hid the shoreline. The only channel markers were natives positioned in the water by "Bish" Silvester to mark each bend in the river. Boles longed for the days of neatly numbered "red nuns" as he tried to meet the challenge of picking out a black man in a black river on a black night.

Now they were off the mouth of the river, bobbing in the waters of The Slot. Here they waited and waited for some sign of the rescue ships. Once they heard the whine of destroyer blowers and vessels going by at high speed, then came a few flares and explosions. Japanese ships were apparently on the prowl, sniffing trouble. Then it was dark again, and the wait continued.

On shore Major Kelly also felt the strain of the long wait. Finally he slipped away from his defense line and consulted with Chew. If the ships didn't come soon, it would be dawn, and they couldn't risk staying here during the day. They began discussing the possibility of returning to camp.

Twelve miles up the coast at Paraso Bay, Bausewine's group was to have a long night, too. The rescue was set for 2 A.M. on the sixteenth, and at midnight Josselyn pushed off in a large canoe to guide in the rescuers. With him went three natives and Bill Dupay, to help make contact. For the next two hours they bobbed up and down in the empty night a mile or so offshore. Then, toward 2 A.M., they spotted the shadowy forms of several blacked-out ships approaching through the dark. There was no clue whether they were friend or foe, but Josselyn hopefully flashed a series of *R*'s—the recognition signal.

On shore George Bausewine and the others restlessly waited as the hours ticked by. He hoped for the best, but he had always been fatalistic about the group's chances. That Rear Admiral Kelly Turner, commander of the area's amphibious forces, would send three thousand men in ten destroyers to rescue them was a thought that had never occurred to him.

From the start Kelly Turner was determined to rescue the *Helena* survivors on Vella Lavella. It was more than a matter of saving 165 good men; it was important to the whole Navy's morale. As he explained, "It means a lot to know that if the worst happens and you get blown off your ship and washed ashore somewhere, the Navy isn't going to forget you."

But how to do the job? PBY's, submarines, PT-boats—all the usual ways were out. They just couldn't hold enough men. Ships were clearly the answer, and the destroyer-transports *Dent* and *Waters* seemed the best bet. Painted a mottled jungle green, these APD's (as they were called) had the right size and speed, with crews specially trained in amphibious operations—and looking at it one way, this was just an amphibious operation in reverse.

Protecting the two APD's was the problem. They were lightly armed, and this would be the Navy's deepest penetration yet into enemy-controlled waters. The Japanese not only held Vella Lavella, but had airstrips on Bougainville and on Ballale Island, plus their anchorage in the Shortland Islands only sixty miles away.

Kelly Turner took few chances. As the *Dent* and *Waters* steamed toward Vella Lavella on the afternoon of July 15, they were escorted by four destroyers under Captain Thomas J. Ryan. Out of sight but very much in the picture were four more destroyers under Captain Francis X. McInerney. They would hover in The Slot during the pickup, ready to intercept any Japanese ships coming down from the Shortlands. McInerney was in overall charge of the operation.

Midnight, and Ryan's six ships, coming up from the south, entered Vella Gulf. The moon was full, and it was hard to believe they had not been sighted. At 1:12 a white flare went up from Vella off to port, and the crews braced for an attack. Nothing happened. Five minutes later, a red parachute flare shot up from Kolombangara on the starboard side. Again the men steeled themselves; again nothing happened.

At 1:30 they were off Paraso Bay. Now the destroyer *Taylor* turned inshore, and using both lead lines and sophisticated depth-finding equipment, guided the *Dent* and *Waters* into the bay toward the mouth of the Paraso River. The other three destroyers formed the inner screen, patrolling the bay's entrance. Ten miles out, Captain McInerney's four destroyers took their station as the outer screen. A Japanese patrol plane spotted them and dropped a few bombs that fell harmlessly into the water. Otherwise

41

no interference. Their luck was holding.

On the bridge of the *Dent* Commander John D. Sweeney peered into the darkness, trying to follow the movements of the *Taylor* just ahead. He was commodore of the two APD's and gloried in the code name PLUTO. The *Taylor*, with deeper draft, finally reached a point where she couldn't go any farther. She backed away, signaling over the radio, "PLUTO, you're on your own. Good luck."

The *Dent* and *Waters* crept on a few yards, now so close to land that the shadows of the trees hid the shoreline. Suddenly a signalman called, "Captain, there's a light." Sweeney rushed to the wing of the bridge, looked down, and saw a canoe coming out of the dark. A voice in the canoe called, "I am the gunner of the *Helena*!"

When he called the words out, Bill Dupay still wasn't sure whether these darkened ships creeping into the bay were American or Japanese; he simply decided to take a chance. It worked out, and a minute later the canoe was alongside the *Dent*. He and Josselyn clambered aboard.

The *Dent* and *Waters* now hove to and lowered their Higgins boats. Each ship contributed three, and with Josselyn acting as pilot, the little armada chugged through the reefs to the river mouth, where Bausewine's party was waiting.

In a remarkably short time the boats were all back, and Henry Josselyn now went to the bridge of the *Dent*. Sweeney needed no introduction: he had landed Josselyn a year earlier at Tulagi as a guide with the Marines. To his surprise, the commander now learned that these were less than half the men to be evacuated. No one had briefed him about the second group at Lambu Lambu. He didn't know the coast, and in a few hours it would be daylight.

Don't worry, said Josselyn, he'd guide the ships there. Sweeney advised the screen, and the rescue fleet got under way. Toward 4 A.M. the *Dent* poked into Lambu Lambu Cove, and the bridge quickly spotted a light off the starboard bow flashing the *Helena*'s number 50. The *Dent* flashed a long red light back and cut her engines.

Warren Boles never did see the answering red flash. He only knew that these ships were coming from the "wrong" direction. Nobody had told him that the rescue fleet was going to Paraso first, and he was expecting ships from the southeast, up from Tulagi. He flashed his signal anyhow, but when he failed to catch the answer, he really began to worry. He wondered whether to turn tail and run for shore, but finally decided the die was cast—rescue was now or never—so he kept flashing his light.

Pretty soon he heard the sound of small-craft engines, then in the darkness a British voice sang out, "Hello there." It was Henry Josselyn in the first of the *Dent*'s Higgins boats. Skippered by Ensign Rollo H. Nuckles, the boat drew alongside the canoe, and Boles climbed aboard. It wasn't easy: the ten-day ordeal had taken its toll. He had a gimpy leg, and a gash on his left arm was so badly infected that the arm hung useless by his side.

With Boles acting as pilot, the landing craft continued on, traveling in a column of six. Somehow he found the mouth of the river, and then began the difficult business of navigating the various bends and turns. The live "channel markers" were still in place, but it was debatable whether they were more a help than a hazard.

At last the boats reached the rickety dock where Chew's group was waiting. The pier could handle only one boat at a time; so they took turns going in. As each was loaded, Jack Chew stood at the edge of the water, counting the men scrambling aboard. Nearly every one paused to shake hands with some native, and many of the men handed out all the cash they had. Far more useful on Vella Lavella was the sheath knife that Chesleigh Grunstad gave a native he had grown to know and like.

Through it all the men kept as quiet as possible. They were always half-convinced that the Japanese lay just out of sight, waiting to pounce. A Chinese baby started to cry, and to Ted Blahnik, "it was the loudest noise I ever heard."

Soon the crowd on the dock thinned down to a few dozen, and Major Kelly began to pull in his Irregulars. As they prepared to board the last boat, one by one they handed their assorted rifles and pistols to the native scouts. Kelly watched the transfer of the last weapon; then he, too, stepped aboard.

As senior officer, Chew was the last to go. He conveyed his thanks to Josselyn, whom he had just met, and turned to Silvester. It was hard to find the right words, and maybe a small gesture conveyed his gratitude better than anything he could say. Jack Chew, that most superstitious of old sailors, handed Bish his most prized talisman of all, his lucky silver dollar.

The Higgins boats got under way; Silvester and Josselyn gave a final wave and faded into the bush.

On the *Dent* and *Waters* the rescued men swarmed below to rediscover a host of basic pleasures—good chow, cigarettes, hot water, soap, clean underwear. In the wardroom of the *Waters* Jack Chew downed five bowls of pea soup, then enjoyed the luxury of a real shower. He was too excited to sleep; so he wandered into the wardroom again and talked the rest of the night away.

Daylight, July 16, and American fighters from New Georgia appeared overhead. The rescue fleet pounded on toward Tulagi, out of harm's way at last. On the bridge of the *Dent* Commander Sweeney wondered what sort of men did the things Henry Josselyn did. Their parting gave him little clue. Sweeney had offered to take Josselyn to Tulagi, but he said no, there was still work to be done. Then Sweeney offered him some cases of canned food, but Josselyn again said no: the natives might leave the empty cans around, giving away his position.

"Can't we do anything for you?" Sweeney asked.

"Yes," said Josselyn, "I could use a couple of pairs of black socks, some Worcestershire sauce, and a few bars of candy."

The astonishing heroism of a handful of such men as Josselyn and Silvester is described in Walter Lord's forthcoming history, Lonely Vigil: Coastwatchers of the Solomons, *from which this story is excerpted. The new book, Mr. Lord's tenth, will be published soon by The Viking Press.*

Still wearing life jackets, a group of grimy, unshaven, ragged, and joyous survivors of the Helena *pose for a photograph aboard the rescue ship after their dramatic escape from Vella Lavella on July 16, 1943.*

WILLIAM SHROUT. *Life* MAGAZINE © TIME INC.

The Big Thicket

A Last Link with the Living Frontier

The Big Thicket is an ecological wonder. This dense forest, sprawling between the Sabine and Trinity rivers in east Texas, constitutes a natural crossroads for plant and animal species from almost every part of the country. No less remarkable is the pioneer way of life that still flourishes where the dwindling generation of settlers' descendants live in the Thicket's leafy shadow, just fifty miles from downtown Houston.

When the first pioneers pushed toward Texas in the 1820's and '30's, the Big Thicket was a formidable green barrier, sixty miles thick and one hundred miles long. Most were content to go around. Those who hacked their way through it never forgot the experience. "This day passed through the thickest woods I ever saw," wrote one exhausted settler in 1835. "It perhaps surpasses any country for brush."

Indeed it did—and does. "Big Thicket" is actually a misnomer, for its green fastness once harbored all sorts of wilderness terrain: tall groves of virgin pine and cypress; thickly shaded hardwood forests; flower-filled meadows; impenetrable black-water swamps festooned with vines and Spanish moss. Even the Alabama and Coushatta Indians who hunted the Thicket's deer and bear shunned its deepest reaches, and, except for isolated bands of outlaws and runaway slaves, the settlers who stayed here built their cabins around the tiny towns that sprang up along the fringes of the forest.

The society they spawned was close-knit: perhaps half of the Thicket's surviving residents are related by blood. Their accents and ways of doing things were those of the southern Appalachians from which they came. Left behind by the westward wave of emigration, the people of the Big Thicket were independent, wary of strangers, and generally law abiding—though law in the formal sense took a long time in coming. Above all, they were self-sufficient. Even the Civil War passed them by: when the call went out for soldiers for the Confederate Army, many took to the woods for the duration.

Over the years the Thicket has changed more than have its people. Lumbermen began to float mammoth pine and cypress logs down its rivers during the 1850's, and later built sawmills to turn out millions of railroad ties and barrel staves. They felled thousands of acres of ancient trees, and poisoned thousands more so that today only regimented rows of fast-growing commercial pine can survive where hardwood forests had stood since the Ice Age.

And while the Thicket retreated steadily before the logger's axe, other outsiders made inroads. The turn-of-the-century oil strikes transformed small settlements into boom towns; rice farmers flooded portions of the forest; developers eager to house suburbanites bulldozed still more.

By the early 1970's, the great forest seemed doomed. Then, through the doggedness of private citizens and conservation groups, some eighty-five thousand acres were set aside as perpetual wilderness.

But saving a fragment of wilderness is easy compared to saving a vanishing way of life. Change is coming fast to the people of the Big Thicket: television beams in jarring images of the outside world; the impatient young drift away to the big towns. More and more it is the old men and women who remain, clinging to their memories and to what is left of their tangled forest home.

Over the last nine years, naturalists Campbell and Lynn Loughmiller have roamed the region, seeking to record the essence of the world of the Big Thicket pioneers before it vanishes. From thousands of hours of taped reminiscences they have skillfully assembled a book, *Big Thicket Legacy,* just published by the University of Texas Press. On the following pages we hear the voices of people whose daily lives are still filled with the sounds and color of the American frontier.

—G.C.W.

PHOTOGRAPHS OF BIG THICKET RESIDENTS ARE BY CAMPBELL AND LYNN LOUGHMILLER. ALL COLOR PHOTOGRAPHS ARE BY BLAIR PITTMAN, EXCEPT WHERE NOTED.

Brown Wiggins
Logger, grocer

A lot of the Indians came into the Thicket after their meat. They lived at the Indian Village, east of Livingston, and they'd come about twice a year when I was small. They'd generally come in the spring, along in April, and in late September. The main game they wanted was deer, and they knew where all the springs and water holes was. There was only one in the bunch that could talk. The men would ride the little ponies and the squaws would walk. If they had babies they'd carry them on their backs in a sack. And quite a lot of poor little dogs came along, so poor you could count the joints in their tails.

Hog grease was what they wanted. And they'd come and line up crossways in our front yard and go to humming, no tune to it, sort of a chant. This was their way of announcing their presence. This was when they'd be on their way to hunt. If we had a dirty potato patch or cotton patch or something, they'd grab the hoes and hoe it out, and they'd do it good. Then my father, we had a smokehouse about twelve by fifty hanging full of cured meat, and my father would give them two or three of the shoulders, and we had lard put up in buckets. He'd give them some of that and a sack of salt, and they'd pull out. This old Indian would say, "You come." He wanted us to come to his camp, and the only way you would ever find his camp, about every fifty yards he'd hack a bush and just let it fall over, but as a general thing they went pretty straight.

And those old Indians, before they started back, they'd get that deer meat and put it on a scaffold and build a smoke under it in the sun. And the women would watch it while the men would hunt. That venison is all lean meat and it will dry as hard as a piece of wood. They'd put that in a sack and carry it back home. We fixed a lot of it that way. If you want to cook it tomorrow, you throw it in a pan of water tonight, and tomorrow it makes the best hash you ever had almost; it's mighty nice.

Ellen Walker
Widow, onetime cutter of railroad ties

My daddy built our house out of pine, hand-hewed logs, notched and fitted and leveled. The floor was three inches thick and hewed out of logs. The kitchen wasn't built on to the rest of the house but was connected by a shed. It was built out of round logs, not hewed. The floor was red clay, built up about twelve inches higher than the ground. They'd always have a mudcat chimney, take about a day to build, neighbors help. Women would cook and men built the chimney. I stayed right there till I was twenty years old, when I married and moved to Saratogie, and I've been here ever since.

Uncle Bud and Uncle Jim was our closest neighbors, six miles to their house. Uncle Bud hunted a lot. He called me to the gate one morning, said, "Come here, I got a purty for ya." I went out there and he reached back in his saddle pocket, and he had a little old bear about ten inches long. The old mama bear had one of his dogs hugged up and about to kill it. He run in and jabbed his gun in her mouth and shot her, and the print of her teeth was on each side of his Winchester. She had two little cubs in her bed and he carried 'em home and raised 'em. They'd walk on their hind feet and hold up a broom just like somebody.

We raised what we eat, had a garden. Always had a patch o' corn and sweet potatoes, sugar cane and maybe some peanuts. We'd raise peas and when they'd get dry, ma'd put somethin' in 'em to keep the weevils out. Had all kinds of meat: venison, turkey, squirrel. We'd cure bear meat. You can cure it just as good as you can hog meat, and you can season with it, too. You can eat all you want of it and drink the lard, and it won't make you sick. Now old summer bear, they ain't fit to eat; they're pore; they stink. But in the wintertime, they're big and fat and they're good. I liked bear meat, but in the summertime, I wanted venison. We could get that any day we wanted it, and turkey too. I loved squirrel just any time, and we eat rabbit in the wintertime.

COPYRIGHT © 1977 BY THE UNIVERSITY OF TEXAS PRESS

Lance Rosier
Self-taught naturalist

The people here was very poor and some of them didn't want to fight for the Negroes [in the Civil War]. You see the wealthy people here was the only ones who had Negro slaves. So when the war started they said, "Well, I'll just go out here in the woods and stay." These people was called jayhawkers. They had everything to eat without worrying about anything—plenty of game and fish. Their people would have corn ground and carry it out to a big forked oak tree right on the edge of a pond and put it in the fork of that tree. To keep it from getting wet, they had a doeskin they put over it. The pond to this day is known as Doeskin Pond. They'd cut down a tree and rob it, get all kinds of honey. Where Honey Island is now there was two big pear trees and they taken some plank and built a table between those two trees. They'd put all the honey and deer and stuff that they wanted carried off on this table. Their people would come and get this produce, carry it to Beaumont and sell it, and buy their tobacco or whatever they had to have. They'd take it out to Doeskin Pond and put it up in the tree, or leave it on the table at Honey Island.

The [Confederate] government would send soldiers in here and try to get them out, but they never could get them because they kept guards stationed around and when they'd see them coming, they'd leave their hideout. The soldiers would search everywhere for them and never could find them. They never would go in or out the same way. They never would break a limb off. They wouldn't leave any sign where they went into their hideout.

They caught a few jayhawkers one time and carried them to Woodville and put them in jail on the courthouse square, and put guards all around there to guard them. Somebody, in order to free the jayhawkers, brought a lot of whiskey and the guards all got drunk. Then someone got a fiddle and started playing. Mr. Warren Collins began a jig and was entertaining everybody, and all the time he was dancing, everyone was leaving, one at a time. When the party was over there was no jayhawkers left and the guards was too drunk to find them.

* * *

Before the oil boom in 1903 just about a dozen people lived in Saratoga. Where the old oil field was, my Aunt Mat rented a five-room house, took out all the partitions except her room, and turned it into a kitchen and dining room. She got a lot of tents and cots and put them up in front for people to sleep. She ran this place until she was able to save two thousand dollars. Then she built a hotel. The lumber had to be hauled on wagons from four miles on the other side of Kountze. It was built out of longleaf, heart pine. The outside wall was made out of planks that extended the full distance from the ground to the roof and it was 2½ stories high. That's the kind of timber that was here in those days. It cost a thousand dollars to build it and a thousand dollars to furnish it. She had fourteen rooms and could seat thirty in the dining room. She served family style and it was two bits a meal. Room and board was three dollars a week. The train came in at eleven o'clock and left at two. When the salesmen came in on the train—they called them drummers—they had such a short time to see anybody, she let them eat first so they could catch the train at two. Then the roughnecks and everybody else would eat. She had to clean the rooms up two times a day, once for the ones that slept in the daytime, and then for the ones who slept at night.

People managed just any way they could. Some of the houses was built out of pasteboard boxes, and those who couldn't buy tents even camped out under the pine trees. They weren't here to stay, just to make money, come for just a while and then leave.

About every other building was a saloon, and somebody got killed nearly every day. I heard my aunt say a lot of times, "Well, if somebody is going to get killed, I wish I could see it." She was going to buy some groceries for dinner one day and she passed in front of the saloon. As she did, a man ran out right in front of her and somebody in the saloon shot him—and he fell right in front of her! She just stepped over him and went on. She said she didn't ever want to see anybody else killed.

Big Thicket dwellers share both its beauty and its menace. The grass-pink (center left), a member of the orchid family, and the Indian pipe (bottom left) are two of over 2,000 flowering species to flourish here. The brilliance of the fly mushroom (center) belies its toxicity. Far right (top to bottom): a timorous white-tailed fawn drinks at streamside; a cardinal sits out a rainstorm; a razorback sow flees a pack of "cur dogs" bred for the chase; and an alligator coolly waits for prey. At top left, next to the bucket, is a hunter's trophy—the sun-bleached jawbone of a razorback boar, its tushes capable of laying open brave dog and foolhardy hunter alike.

PERRY SHANKLE, JR.

A. Randolph Fillingim
Trapper, farmer

This country could get wet! The first thing that comes to my mind when I think about Sour Lake is mud. If you got off the boards they used for sidewalks, you'd bog halfway to your knees. It was just a tremendous mud-lolly. One time a tractor was coming down the street pulling a load, during the oil boom, and it started bogging, and went down farther and farther, until finally the top of the tractor was even with the ground, right at the main intersection. The owners built a little barricade out of two-by-fours around the top of it, so nobody would run over it, and left it there from May until July. When the ground got dried out some, they went in there and dug it out, and it ran all right.

The people, of course, they wanted a better living, so some of them started making whiskey after they found out they could dispose of it and make money, 'cause most all of the people in our settlement either made it, or sold it, or drank it, except my father and my brother and me. Our family didn't make it, and didn't sell it, but our neighbors did and we treated them just like we did before.

A quart of whiskey would sell for ten dollars a quart, forty dollars a gallon. Our neighbors told us they could take a hundred pounds of corn chops and fifty pounds of sugar and put it in about a 50-gallon water barrel and ferment it, and distill it, and get 2½ gallons of good corn whiskey. Well, that would be a hundred dollars for one sack of corn chops and fifty pounds of sugar, and just a little trouble; so it was one of the most tempting things anybody ever had to overcome if they needed money to take care of their family.

Three of our neighbors made whiskey—a man and his son and another man. They had the reputation of making the most and the best whiskey, so they made pretty good money out of it. At first he would pass by our house, and we could see the sugar and corn chops in his little mule wagon. The first thing we noticed, he bought a new wagon, and a few months later we heard something come buzzing down the old country road—just a wagon trail is all it was—and it was a shiny Model T Ford, brand new.

P. O. (Phil) Eason
Pentecostal minister, hunter

When I was a boy we would have parties and all meet at some family's house and play games until late at night. There would always be refreshments. The neighbors lived maybe three miles apart, just dim wagon roads connecting them. Now these parties would be in full swing until twelve or one o'clock, and then everybody would get ready to go home. If the boys had brought the girls to the party they would then walk home with them. This was the best part of the get-together, and it was a most pleasant distance we traveled. If you have never been out in the Big Thicket at night, you don't know what a dark night can be like. We didn't know what a flashlight was. We had the old kerosene lantern in those days, but what young man would carry a lantern in one hand while piloting a young lady home with the other? We'd rather take a chance on being caught by a panther or bit by a rattlesnake. Of course this was the courage we had while escorting the young lady home, but when you started back and heard animals in the bushes, and so dark you couldn't see the ground in front of you, it was something else. Many nights a pack of wolves serenaded me with their lonesome howl, and it would make my hair stand up, give me goose pimples all over.

The Thicket has been my life. I've hunted just about every animal in the woods, but it wasn't just the hunting. I just enjoy being in the woods. There's hardly a time of the year you won't find flowers in bloom, and in the spring it's just a sight when the haws and the sweet bay and magnolias, and berries and jasmine and wild plum and dogwood are in bloom. My favorite is the wild honeysuckle.

I got out of the hospital Friday and took a walk in the woods Saturday, just back of the house here. Of course, I was just about dead when I got back. The doctor told me to stay inside, but I can get a couple of squirrels for dinner without leaving my backyard. They bark at my puppy dog I got tied back there. And I'd be surprised if I couldn't jump a deer a quarter of a mile from the house. I'm not able to walk that much yet, but my boy's going to take me to a deer stand in the morning. Doc wouldn't like it but I don't think it'll hurt me. If I die, I'll die happy.

PURITAN PICTURES presents

TIM McCOY in

"Lightnin' BILL CARSON"

with
LOIS JANUARY · REX LEASE

DIRECTED BY
SAM NEWFIELD

PRODUCED BY
SIG NEUFELD and LESLIE SIMMONDS

High Eagle

The Many Lives of Colonel Tim McCoy

An interview by Darryl Ponicsan

Who is Colonel Tim McCoy? He is the last surviving cowboy hero of the silent screen. His contemporaries—Tom Mix, Hoot Gibson, Buck Jones, Ken Maynard, Fred Thompson, Harry Carey, and lesser lights—are all gone, some of them for many years. Only McCoy remains, now as then solidly sure of the choices in life and decisively intolerant of injustice.

Timothy John Fitzgerald McCoy was born in Saginaw, Michigan, in 1891. At age eighteen he went west, while the West was still a proving ground for young men of grit. He learned the skills of a cowboy, homesteaded in Wyoming, and became a rancher of sorts. The Indians of the area, the Arapahoes and Shoshones, saw in him a man of their own spirit. He learned their language, including the sign language, and was given by them the name "High Eagle."

His career was a varied one. He served during World War I as a Cavalry officer and mustered out at the end of the war with the rank of lieutenant colonel. For a time he served as an aide to General Hugh L. Scott, an old Indian fighter, and when Scott was appointed head of the Board of Indian Commissioners, both he and the Arapahoes wanted McCoy to become an Indian agent. McCoy declined: "The bureaucratic restrictions would almost certainly have ruined our friendship."

It was his expertise in the language and customs of American Indians that first brought him to Hollywood in 1923 as technical adviser for the filming of the epic The Covered Wagon, directed by James Cruze. In addition, he acted as liaison between the director and the hundreds of Indian extras. When the picture was released in Los Angeles, at Graumann's Theater, McCoy and his Indians performed a live prologue on stage. The picture, and the prologue, proved so popular that both ran for some eight months before moving on to Europe. MGM, attracted by McCoy's rugged good looks, military bearing, and no-nonsense style, signed him as their first cowboy hero star, at an age when most current stars are feeling the pangs of professional mortality.

The Western was the first (though temporary) casualty of the advent of sound pictures, and most silent-screen cowboys, including Tim McCoy, found themselves suddenly at the end of their bright careers, with no more to show for their stardom than the strength of character they tried to instill in their young admirers and discovered in themselves. McCoy went home to his ranch in Wyoming, content with his moment of glory. But soon he was called back again, first to make a talking serial at Universal, The Indians Are Coming, and later to do a series of sound Westerns at Columbia.

During the 1935 through 1938 seasons, the last golden age for American circuses, McCoy went on the road with Ringling Brothers-Barnum and Bailey and gave the children of the country a chance to see one of their heroes in the flesh. The tours were enormously successful, so much so that he was persuaded to put together his own Wild West show and take to the road. It was a disaster. To recoup his losses, he went back to Hollywood to do a series of Westerns with Buck Jones and Raymond Hatton for Monogram Pictures called The Rough Riders.

World War II took him away from films for the duration, and when he returned he became involved in early television as the host of his own show, for which he won an Emmy. Since then he has taken parts in occasional movies, the most memorable being that of a Cavalry colonel in Around the World in Eighty Days.

At the age of seventy-one McCoy joined the Tommy Scott Wild West Show, displaying his virtuosity with a gun and a bullwhip, and toured on the road into his eighties. Today he spends his time writing his autobiography (to be published in the late fall) with the help of his son Ronald in Nogales, Arizona, where the following interview took place during the last weekend in October, 1976.

A McCoy movie poster, 1936

Colonel, you're eighty-five years old now and you qualify as a survivor in every aspect of that word. Do you feel any sense of victory?

No, I have no sense of victory, but there is a little bit of satisfaction in realizing that I am one of the few men that I know of who has done everything he ever wanted to in life. I have no unfulfilled ambitions. I have no frustrations. Any time an idea ever came to me, I made it come true.

Looking back, which one gives you the most satisfaction?

Oh, how can I tell? You see, it depends on whether one can get enthusiastic about anything or interested enough. And all of these things that I've done have been most interesting, from the days that I was a cowboy on the range. I wanted to be a cowboy, so I became a cowboy and it was great. I wanted to be an Army officer and I became an officer. I have two wars behind me and I am now a retired colonel of the Cavalry with over thirty years' service. Motion pictures is a thing that just happened because of my Indians, and once I got into that I enjoyed it.

Let's talk about all those things. Now, you came out West when you were no more than a boy. You were eighteen, weren't you?

Yes, that's about right.

What was your dream when you set out on that journey as an eighteen-year-old?

Well, I wanted to be a cowboy. I'd been interested in the West. I'd seen the cowboys who had come east with wild horses and broke them out, and I'd get right down in the middle of them when I was just a kid. I was able to rope and ride. Of course, every kid rode because they used to ship these wild horses back from the Western country and break them to sell to guys on drays, carts, and what not. Every kid would be down there among the cowboys. Well, just to see them wasn't enough for me, and it wasn't long before I had my hand on a rope, working along with them. Because of those cowboys I turned west. I wanted to be like them.

You just came out and started working as a ranch hand?

I came out there and went to work as a ranch hand, that's right.

And just learned the skills?

Don't you see, that's the thing. Now, most people think that a cowboy, you just start right off and you're a top cowboy. Well, you've got to serve your apprenticeship; you know, you've got to pay your dues first. You start at the bottom. I'll never forget Ross Santee, the Western artist. I was back East visiting with Frazier Hunt, the author, and we got to talking about the West, so I happened to say to Ross, "Well there was this particular time I was wrangling horses on the roundup . . . ," and Ross said, "What did you say?" I said, "I was wrangling horses." And he got up and he said, "May I shake you by the hand? You're the first son-of-a-bitch who ever came out of the West that wasn't a top hand all his life."

Can you describe the nature of the American cowboy during the early years of this century? What was he like?

Well, he was just another fellow who made his living riding a horse. That's about the only way to describe him. He worked livestock and rode the range.

It was an unusual way of life. It was a hard way of life, wasn't it?

But it was so exciting. There was always something to do. You didn't know whether you were going to get your neck broke in the next minute or what was going to happen to you. But when you're young nothing is tough or hard for you. You roll out your bedroll on the ground—it might rain on you, it might snow on you, but young fellas can take it, you see. When I think of it now, I think it's appalling. The idea of putting in at roundup time about sixteen or eighteen hours a day in the saddle. Who wants to ride down three horses?

In those days, there was still a West to come to. When did the West cease to be a magnet for adventurous young men?

Well, it was fading when I first came to it.

What were the signs of the fading?

So many small ranches being taken up. Homesteaders cut up the big open range a lot, and when a fellow took up a homestead he had to make certain improvements on it, so one of the first and easiest things to do was put a barbed-wire fence around it. Well, that interfered with your cattle running for so many miles. When I first came out, in certain parts of the country that I worked in out there, heavens, we could trail our beef cattle for a hundred miles to the railroad at shipping time in the fall. Toward the end, though, it go so it was a little difficult to find a way to follow the creeks down and get to the railroad without having to run over all these little old ranchers that had their barbed wire up around you. So I would say that that was the beginning of the breaking up of the Old West.

Nowadays men seem wracked by a sense of alienation. Did the cowboys have any of this in your day? I mean, what did you worry about as a young cowboy?

I'm trying to comprehend what you mean by alienation. You were never quite alone. You rode very seldom alone. You were generally in pairs, or on roundups there would be twelve, fifteen, twenty of you. But even so, you had the whole country . . . you had the mountains, streams . . . there was always enough to occupy you. I'll say this when you ask that question. There was one thing that a cowboy never heard about and that was a psychiatrist.

He had no need for a psychiatrist?

He was not disturbed mentally at all. Of course, most of

them didn't have any mentality, I guess, or they wouldn't have been cowboys. I can remember riding along all by myself. You have a chance to let your imagination run wild with you and your imagination takes you right out of the saddle—talk about the knight in shining armor, you're that fellow. It might be as you're riding a great distance that you could sort of imagine that the next bend around the next spur of the mountain over there you're going to run into some gal who is just out visiting from the East, visiting on some ranch, and you're going to run into her and she's going to be charming and isn't that going to be fun!

And you just kept on riding—right into World War I, then Hollywood, and then the Wild West show. You know, Colonel, the old Wild West shows and circuses abounded with colonels and majors, and captains, but in your case the title is authentic. You earned it in World War I?

World War I and, of course, I went to World War II. I was a lieutenant colonel at the end of World War I. And I became a brigadier general when I was adjutant general of Wyoming, but my real permanent rank was full colonel—Cavalry. That's what I'm retired as.

Did you see a lot of action in World War I?

Well, you always see a certain amount. You know the odd thing about wars? The only things you ever talk about or think about or remember are the funny things that happened.

What are some of the funny things?

Well, once I was coming back to Washington on a job during World War II and we landed in the Azores early in the morning. We went in to get shaved and cleaned up and have breakfast while they were servicing our plane. I came out and as I was coming over toward our plane, this sergeant in charge of the ground crew came up and clicked and saluted, and he said, "Pardon me, sir, but isn't this Colonel McCoy?"

And I said, "Yes."

"Well," he said, "I've helped you a lot."

"Where did you ever serve under me?" I asked him.

"Oh," he said, "I never served under you, but the small town that I lived in back in Indiana . . . there's a small picture house there and it had a little balcony, and every Saturday I sat right in the front row of that balcony up there and I had a slingshot and a pocketful of iron staples, and every time the villains got anywhere near you, I shot the hell out of them."

Are you able to appreciate from your vantage point the enormous influence you had on children?

Do you know that I get more darn fan mail now? I don't know why. I wish I had gotten that much twenty years ago. Well, they send me posters of the theater to autograph. I've got one over here on my desk. They put the damn things out as postcards. You see . . . this one's a honey. Look at that

"I wanted to be a cowboy, so I became a cowboy. . . . I wanted to be an Army officer and I became an officer." Above, McCoy stands at ease on his Wyoming ranch in the 1920's; at the top, as a captain of Cavalry, he poses ready to face the Hun, in 1917.

55

one, in big letters, "Starring Tim McCoy." Now look at these tiny little letters, the supporting cast... "John Wayne." I get a kick out of that. They're selling them all over the country. People are sending these things to me to be autographed. I've got some that I haven't even opened because I can see what they are.

What did you do during World War II?

Well, World War II... you see I came back on duty for World War II and, heavens, I was fifty years old.

Which you thought was old at that time?

Well, everybody thought it was old. And, so, well, they asked me what I wanted to do. I said, hell, I wanted to command troops. That's all I ever knew. They said, "Not at your age."

I said, "What do you mean, my age?" I told the adjutant general of the Army in Washington, "Do you realize I've been competing with fellows twenty-five years old for the last twenty-four years?"

"Yes," he said, "but did you ever hear of a thing called War Department policy? You will not command troops after you're forty-five years of age unless you are a general officer."

I said, "Well, how close can I get to the troops?" So they gave me the funniest job in the world. Here I am a cavalryman and they sent me over to the Air Force. But it was a great job. My job was to coordinate the air support for the ground troops, so I could whip back and forth from the Air Force. I lived with the Air Force and they lived all right.

Let me ask you, how did you become so involved with Indians?

Well, you see, I was associated with the Indians out in Wyoming for so long, I could talk to them and they would listen to me and they would ask my advice on things.

As a cowboy you were associated with them?

As a cowboy, because when we were riding cattle the big outfits would arrange to get leases of those vacant Indian lands, big reservations, and run their cattle over them and pay the Indians so much. Those things always had to be handled through the Indian Department, had to be O.K.'d by the agent of that particular reservation, and so the Indians would be asking my advice all the time as to what they should do. I could sit down and counsel and talk to them, you see, and I had to give them my opinion. So the fact was that they wanted my opinion on so many things that finally I had more influence over those Indians than anybody else, so that's about the angle of it. Of course, when I was adjutant general of Wyoming after World War I, well, that gave me a lot of latitude and I could get out among them and do about as I pleased.

You became adjutant general having served as an aide to General Hugh L. Scott, isn't that right?

He was chief of staff of the Army and he was about the last of the old-time Indian fighters who were still on active service. And he was chief of staff up until World War I. He was just about to hit the retirement age then, so when his tour of duty was up he became a commissioner of Indian Affairs, and of course I was a protégé of his.

What was it about the American Indian that appealed to you?

There was great *sympatico*. I think I could sum it up best by what old Chief Goes In Lodge said one time. He was an Arapaho. He said, "Long time ago, you must have been an Injun." I guess that's the answer.

In another life?

Maybe in another life. That's what he meant. I could talk to them, understood them, felt as they felt, knew what they were thinking. For that reason, I suppose, that's how I got along with them so well.

Is it true you helped set the record straight on Custer's Last Stand by interviewing Indians who had fought at the Little Bighorn?

Yes. General Scott and I went out and we took with us the last two living scouts who had guided Custer into the Little Bighorn. We followed Custer's march, where he camped, everything he did, got the whole story from those scouts, right up to the beginning of the fight. Of course, they turned and went back; they didn't want to have any part in what was going to take place, because they could see it. They tried to warn Custer, but you couldn't tell him anything.

Then, I was the first one to dig out the fact that there were five Arapahoes in that fight. I dug that out one night sitting in a powwow with a bunch of Arapaho Indians down along the Little Wind River. They started telling me that Old Water Man was in that fight. I sort of scoffed at it because every Indian and his brother was in that fight. Practically all of them killed Custer. When they described Custer and described the fight, you could tell they didn't know what they were talking about. So I was a little bit dubious about it, but they said Water Man and Left Hand, who were still alive, were both in that fight. So I took a stick of sagebrush and cleared a space on the ground and I drew the Bighorn River and the Little Horn and I started asking questions of Water Man. Where was the village? Where did Custer come from? And so on and so on... and by God he knew. So I arranged then to get him in to get his story rather than having to tell it myself. I arranged to have him come into the town of Riverton, Wyoming, and one night I got a hold of Left Hand. I didn't get them together, you see. I brought Water Man in one night and Left Hand another night, and in order that no one would have to take my word for it, I got an interpreter and court stenographer and I did one of these question/answer things that we're doing here and I got a transcript of this whole blasted thing. So I got it from Water Man one night and Left Hand the next night. And I could tell they knew what they were talking about.

"We're always talking about our honor and our American way of doing things and we have never kept a single promise or a single treaty we ever made with the Indian." At left, McCoy is seen in 1924 with Wovoka, the Nevada Paiute shaman whose ghost-dance religion burned itself out at the "battle" of Wounded Knee in 1890. At top right, McCoy and General Hugh L. Scott line up in 1926 with some Montana Blackfeet; directly above, McCoy is seen with the Indians used in his living prologue to The Iron Horse, 1925.

ALL FROM THE COLLECTION OF COLONEL TIM MCCOY

In a recent book, the point is made that many of Custer's men committed suicide out of a pathological fear of being captured by the Indians, and apparently the Indians watched on bewildered as Custer's troops killed each other and themselves. What do you think of that?

I don't buy that at all. Those fellows were too damn busy even to try to kill themselves.

Too busy fighting?

Ha! Too busy trying to make their damn rifles work.

What do you mean?

Toward the end of the Civil War we had gotten a new rifle, the first of the repeating rifles for the Army. It was called the Spencer and it had a tubular magazine that you pushed into the butt. It fired seven shots and that was the first repeating rifle or carbine. The Cavalry was armed with it first. The Indians used to say about it: "That gun, you load it on Saturday, it shoots all week." You see, it held seven shots. It was used very successfully by Custer's division. They were armed with it at Appomattox, for instance, so that the fire power for that one outfit was as much as Lee had in his whole army. But after the war, when somebody wanted to adopt that carbine for the Cavalry, these old fuddy-duddies in Washington, the old-timers in the War Department, said: No, no, these fellows don't know how to handle arms well enough and they'd shoot away too much ammunition. So they went back to the old trap-door Springfield rifle and carbine. It was single shot. You had to throw open the trap door and it was supposed to eject the shell. Well, the shells that they used in those Civil War guns, both the rifle and the carbine, were copper, and copper is fairly soft. It would expand in the chamber of the gun, and when the shell was ejected the ejector would tear the rim off the cartridge, and the fellows at the Custer fight, as the Indians told me, had their knives out trying to pry these shells out of their guns.

So that they could reload?

Right. Old Left Hand told me that he came up the hill and this soldier was wounded and he handed him his gun, wanted to surrender to him. They didn't understand. You don't surrender to an Indian. And Left Hand said he took the gun, but he couldn't use it because the shell jammed in the chamber.

What do you mean, you don't surrender to an Indian?

Well, because they don't understand surrender. You either fight or you die.

They didn't take prisoners?

No, they weren't taking any prisoners there.

The Arapahoes were the Indians you knew best. What is their condition today?

They're in a bad way. They have nothing. They got the poorest end of a reservation they were not even supposed to be on. In about 1876 they were rounded up and were to be taken to a reservation in Nebraska, near the Sioux. Winter was coming on, so instead of being taken to Nebraska they were dropped with the Shoshones in Wyoming. They asked the chief to take them for the winter, because their moccasins were broken, they were destitute, they had gone on the warpath and had the hell shot out of them. The chief allowed them to stay. The Shoshones had no love for the Arapahoes and the Arapahoes had no love for the Shoshones, but they were taken in, because after all they were Indians and winter was coming. So they were to stay there until spring when their reservation would be ready.

And they were forgotten?

They were forgotten. And the Shoshones had to fight like hell—it was only recently that the government finally paid the Shoshones and bought that corner of the reservation where the Arapahoes were. But they got the worst piece of land and were left there to starve to death, which is what they're doing. And drinking themselves to death, because they have no future, nothing to look forward to.

How do you feel about the way the Indians have been portrayed in films?

I remember my advent into pictures and when I tried to tell a director you don't do it that way . . . this is not the way the Indians fought, for example, the answer was, who will know the difference? And there's your whole answer. That was their attitude.

I remember on *The Covered Wagon* they wanted a bunch of teepees spread in a circle so this council could take place in the center. They wanted all the doorways facing into the center. And I said, "Just a minute, we can't do that." And they said, "Why?"

I said, "The doorways do not all face the center." Sure they do, they said. Look here, see what that means. These Indians, we can have them coming out of all the teepees and they come right out of those doors right into this council. But, I said, "You don't understand. Indians do not pitch their teepees that way. They always pitch their teepees with the door facing the east and you can't get them to do otherwise, because when an Indian steps out of his teepee he has to greet his Father, the Sun, in the morning. You will not get them to do it."

"Well, this is the way we want them," they said.

I said, "I tell you what you do. I'll bring that interpreter over here, you tell him. I'm not going to tell him. They know that I know better. But you tell him exactly how you want the teepees pitched and he'll tell the Indians."

So they spent some time with this interpreter, who listened and said, "Okay, I'll tell them."

They said, "You understand?"

"Yeah, I understand, I'll tell them."

We came out there to look. All those teepees were pitched

with the doorways facing the east and these fellows went nuts. What was the idea? And I said, "Don't you understand? You cannot go against an Indian custom. You say who will know the difference? The Indians will know the difference."

How do you feel about the Indian Movement presently, the surge toward Indians' Rights?

Oh, the Indians' Rights. Now you really would get me into something if you got on that because this white man and his treatment of the Indian has been something that . . . well, I can't even begin to express myself because I go completely overboard when I think about it. But you see, we're always talking about our honor and our American way of doing things and we have never kept a single promise or a single treaty we ever made with the Indian. We make him a treaty and say, this land is yours now as long as the grass shall grow and the waters shall flow. Then a white man comes in and says, look, that whole country over there, in that Wallowa Valley, that's too good to let those damn Indians have. Our whole treatment of the Indian has been one of the greatest scandals that's ever been known. We established the first concentration camp when we put them on reservations.

Wasn't Roosevelt the last President who actually spoke with Indian leaders, Indian chiefs?

Theodore Roosevelt. You see, Roosevelt thought like a Western man because he'd been West when he was young. He was really a Westerner, you might say, and he was an understanding man and he tried, but even though he tried, the machine was too big for any one man. You couldn't go against it. When they made up their minds that they were going to do certain things to the Indians they did them, and that was that and you couldn't do anything about it. That's my opinion of it. Politics, politics. If you could take Washington, D.C., and build a great big barbed-wire fence around it and never let one of those bastards get out of there, why, the country would be better off.

Your first introduction to Hollywood was as a technical adviser for The Covered Wagon. *And then you did a live prologue?*

Yes, I had the live prologue. This was at Graumann's Theater. Not the Chinese one. This was before the Chinese was opened. This was the Egyptian. Sid Graumann had just built it. And the first picture that went in there was Douglas Fairbanks in *Robin Hood. The Covered Wagon* followed Doug in there, and Jesse Lasky asked me if I could come down and bring some Indians and come onto the stage and talk to the audience, tell them about making the picture.

I brought fifty Indians down and we camped them—teepees and all—right in Cahuenga Pass where the freeway goes through now. There was nothing but a dirt road and a streetcar line that ran over to Universal City and a kind of a park, a hollow up there in the timbers. We had all the Indians camped there. Sid threw a whole fence around that thing and made it look like a Washington fort and it was a

"Where everybody else was chewing up all the scenery, I played it down." At the top, Noah Beery dies like a dog in Cornered, *1932. In the middle, Tim McCoy ignores his horse but not Raquel Torres in* The Desert Rider, *1929. At the bottom, a stiff arm and a steely look help thwart the villain of* Outlaw Deputy, *1935.*

great gimmick. So, I stayed there at Hollywood for eight or nine months, and then Lasky sent for me. He said, we're going to open *The Covered Wagon* in London, and we don't know how it will go there, how the British will take it, but if you'll go over there with the Indians I think it would be a great sales point and we might be able to put the picture over. Fine. So I rounded up a fresh bunch of Indians and headed for London. We stayed over there for almost a year. By the time I came back I had a world of publicity, of course, and that's when Metro-Goldwyn signed me up as their only Western star.

What were the working conditions then in Hollywood?

Well, you can understand Garbo saying, "I thank I go home now." Five o'clock, my eye. You worked. We'd probably work out at Chatsworth during the day and come in and work until midnight in the studio. There was no such thing as eight hours. You just worked until they shot everything they could shoot for that day. Oh, they could give you more damned arguments, and here you were dying on your feet, but you'd go in there and work, work, work. It was nothing to work until two o'clock in the morning and then they'd give you a call for eight.

That was six days a week, fifty-two weeks a year, wasn't it?

Fifty-two weeks a year. Six days a week. Sometimes you'd get a breather between pictures.

Most cowboy heroes of that day developed a particular character and played that character in each picture. What was yours like and how did it evolve?

Well, where everybody else was chewing up all the scenery, I played it down. Someone said that I was the master of the offstage entrance, and that was done with a gimmick that I thought of. A fellow was picking on someone in a saloon and you could just hear my voice coming over—they kid me so much about it today—"I wouldn't do that if I were you." And the camera pans over, and there I am in my black outfit standing looking over with that steely look that they talk about. When I think of that "steely look" I have to laugh, because when I first came to MGM they didn't know what to do with me because of these blue eyes. For a close-up they used to hold up black velvet in front of me so that the darkness would reflect in my eyes. If I looked sideways they said I showed too much of the white of the eye. Well, it became my trademark without knowing it. I said, "Heavens, let me play this. Don't bother me. You fellows get in my way with all this stuff. Let me do the scene and then you can see how it looks on the screen." And then I would suddenly turn and look at someone like that and they called it that steely eye.

You mentioned your costume. There has been a lot written about the Western costume and the significance of each costume. Yours was completely black, wasn't it?

Yeah, I never went in for all the flamboyant clothes. I finally went to a beige Stetson, the type of hat that I wore in Wyoming. One of the reasons they wanted me to go to the light hat was they were shooting night scenes and thought they wouldn't see me so well with a black hat on. But I thought the black hat was more effective. Eventually, it was picked up by Hopalong Cassidy. But I originated that black stuff.

Also, the cowboy heroes used to be closely associated with their horses. I don't remember your horse.

I had a palomino horse that the publicity department used to use. Called him Pal. But I never went for that idea of the horse coming and untying the knots that bound me up, and that sort of thing. I tried to play pretty legitimately. Let's put it this way. I used to have a funny feeling and I mentioned it often to the people on the set. I said, "Remember, I got to go back to Wyoming when I finish this picture. I got a ranch up there and I don't want any of that phony business 'cause they're gonna laugh at me when I go home."

W*ell, what was the real cowboy's relationship to his horse?*

That was the thing you got on and rode.

You didn't have to like him, in other words?

No, and the horse didn't like you. I never knew a horse that did like anybody. Don't dare tell it to horse lovers, but a horse isn't too bright. I had the funniest thing happen in the circus. I had a great big palomino stud—he stood seventeen hands high—the dumbest animal I ever knew. He'd ride you right off the side of a roof if you put him over there. So my cowboy would bring him up to me when I was getting ready to go on, and this particular day for my entrance I wore my buckskin jacket. It was made for me by Arapaho squaws, and was smoke-tanned. He smelled that smoked tan and he put his nose right against my chest, and some woman said, "Oh, he knows his master, doesn't he? He loves his master."

I said, Oh, oh, don't forget that one. So what I would do, whenever there were people standing around back there when they brought the horse up, all I'd do is stretch out my arms and he'd come right straight up and put his nose against my chest to smell that smoke. He knows his master! He didn't give a damn about me.

Tell me a little bit about what happened when sound came to motion pictures.

I probably would still be at MGM except for sound. My contract with Metro-Goldwyn-Mayer had an option coming up just at that time, and they said to me, "Look, we can't take up your option because everything is going to be sound and we can't go outdoors with sound." Everything was done on a small boxed-in stage, and in the beginning they didn't even have them soundproofed. They'd have to shoot at night when there was no traffic going by, and they would have to take this microphone and hide it under a vase of flowers or something of that sort and then you'd have to play your scenes in such a way that you had to be turned toward that thing when you read your lines.

My family was in Europe. The kids were all in school in Paris. So I just high-tailed it over and spent that winter in Europe with the family. When I came back I was a forgotten man.

So many of the big cowboy stars like Tom Mix and Hoot Gibson and others made millions and they wound up with little or nothing at the ends of their lives. That obviously won't happen to you.

Well, you know, I used to sort of think to myself, with all my vicissitudes I hoped that when I got older I'd be able to come into Snug Harbor. A lot of those fellows made more money than I did. Mix, for instance, made more money than any of us. But there's a way of pacing yourself and gearing yourself, and I've enjoyed life and I've certainly never been tight. I have no regrets, even with my circus. We dropped a bundle on the circus. I mean I didn't go broke personally, but I lost a bundle and everybody else did who put it in there because it was the biggest Wild West show that had ever taken the road. You could have put Buffalo Bill's show in half of it. And even though that was a financial failure, it was not a failure for me because it satisfied one of the ambitions that I had. I have a facility of when anything happens to me like that I just draw a curtain on it and never look back over my shoulder. All I can say is try to live the best way you can, do the things you want to do, if you have the gall and stupidity and nerve, whatever it happens to be.

You mentioned the failure of your Wild West show. That was after very successful tours with Ringling Brothers from 1935 to 1938, wasn't it?

Yes, and Ringling wanted me to come back but I simply had to take out my own show.

That was the disastrous year for all circuses.

In 1938. Nearly every circus went broke.

What's the explanation for that?

Simple. The people didn't come.

But they did come when you were with Ringling Brothers? I imagine that you drew an awful lot of children to those shows, didn't you?

Oh, yes, those were three great years for me. They were three very prosperous years. We drew children to the show and we drew them to the after show the same way. Those were terrific years.

Did your role as a cowboy hero put upon you a moral responsibility, some sort of obligation to these kids?

I think all of this stuff of feeling that you had to hold yourself up to the kids, I think it's playing scenes with yourself. I really think you're dramatizing yourself a bit when you talk that way about it. I didn't make all the tabloids and the scandal sheets because I didn't live that

"I am one of the few men that I know of who has done everything he ever wanted to in life. I have no unfulfilled ambitions. I have no frustrations." The Colonel today takes his ease in the sun of Nogales, Arizona. "I have," he says, "a bright future behind me."
TERRENCE MOORE

way. But as far as my impact on the kids, that never occurred to me. It was just a matter of personal pride. If I just went out and played myself, why, that was all that I could give the kids.

I notice when you started naming your friends in Hollywood, you didn't include the other cowboy stars—Harry Carey, Art Acord, Buck Jones, Tom Mix...

I knew those fellows.

But you didn't hang around with them?

No, the only time I ever saw half of them was on the set. I never saw them socially, and I am not saying this in a snooty sort of way.

Well, they were a pretty tough crowd.

Yeah, they were. They just weren't my kind of people.

Did your time away during World War II hurt your career in films?

Yes, it practically finished me. I came back and got in touch with my agent and said, well, I'm ready to go to work again. Now, I was the same guy that went off to war and in just as good shape, and what we ran up against was this: "Oh, Tim's been off the screen for a long time."

And I said, "But I've been to war."

"Well, a lot of the guys have been in the war, so what?" That's when I said, "Oh, the hell with it." And I fussed around a bit and I saw this thing television coming on, so I just lowered my head like a buffalo and charged. I got myself a television program that I had for five years, right in Hollywood. I got that Emmy for it, up there on the shelf.

You were almost a pioneer in TV too?

Yeah, I was the first one, I think, that started a one-man show. I had a one-man show but I would gather around me all that bunch of Indians I had used in pictures for years. They were very versatile, and if I wanted to do a thing about the Hopi Indians they were Hopis. If I wanted to do something about the Plains Indians they were Plains Indians. I could go over to the director of the Southwest Museum and borrow anything out of the cases. Maybe if I was doing a Hopi wedding, I had the original Hopi wedding dresses and everything was authentic. Or I might go into guns—Colts and rifles. A teacher told me one time she took a class over to the Southwest Museum, and as they stepped in the door there were some guns on the wall, and a little kid ran right over and he started telling her about the guns. She asked him how he knew all those details. He said, "I saw Tim McCoy on the television." He had learned all about it.

I had prime time. I was on Saturday night at seven o'clock on KNX-TV out there. Well, the guy that took my place was Jackie Gleason.

Would you care to make any observations on the progress of TV between then and now?

Well, I don't like what TV is doing. It's just like the picture business, except it's on a smaller screen. And if someone gets an idea about one picture everybody wants to make another picture just like it.

What are your plans for the future?

I'm exactly like Cal Stuart, a fellow who was in vaudeville years ago, did one of those early New England characters. As he talked he whittled. He's speaking about his son who he sent off to school. He asked him, he said: "Did you go through Algebra?" And the boy said, "If I did it was in the night and I was on the train and I didn't see it." He whittled for awhile and then he said, "The boy has a bright future, behind him." So when you say, what are my plans for the future, I have a bright future behind me.

There is one thing, though. I told you earlier that I have no unfulfilled ambitions, but that isn't exactly true. There's one thing left in my life needs doing, and I'll have a hard time lying still if I don't do it.

A couple of years ago, I drove up through Wyoming and I knew that between Lander and Riverton, right on the edge where St. Steven's Jesuit Mission is, there was an Indian cemetery and a lot of my old friends would be buried there. So I pulled my car off the road and fought my way through the weeds up to this Indian burying ground and I practically wept. Here were these old-time buffalo-hunting Indians, buried in a place that no pet cemetery... of course, pet cemeteries are well kept. Weeds, dirt, beer cans, crosses knocked down, the damnedest looking place I'd ever seen. So I made up my mind that I'm going back up there, get a few friends who will contribute some money, and go on up there and clean up that cemetery and put it back so it is respectable for those Indians to lie in.

I walked around there, through the weeds and the junk, and saw the names of my friends. They Anglicized all of their names. We have taken away not only their culture but even their names. James L. Brown. I said, "For God's sake, that's Jim Lonebear." D. D. Hill—this Indian's name was Drives Downhill. And the one that really got me was Charles Caldwell. He was a big chief in the Arapahoes, Yellow Calf. He's buried under the name of Caldwell. God Almighty!

There is a tombstone up there that is most interesting. Indians that had a little money and had ranches and made the ranching business go, they didn't become wealthy or anything of the sort. But this one is so pathetic. They got a white tombstone and had taken it in and had it carved: "Annie Wise, aged four years, buried in coffin same as a white man." Pretty damn pathetic, isn't it? I've got the priest up there now at the reservation, hunting to find where my old friend Chief Goes In Lodge is buried. I know he's buried out there in that cemetery somewhere. Not even a marker. He's my brother.

A screenwriter and novelist, Darryl Ponicsan is the author of Cinderella Liberty, The Last Detail, *and* Tom Mix Died for Your Sins.

THE WAY I SEE IT

by Bruce Catton

DANIEL KRAMER

Back in the early years of the present century the advertising industry cooked up an art form that had a quaint and brief life.

Which is to say that the industry used to get out pamphlets using fictional situations to draw attention to the merits of the product that was being advertised. These were aimed straight at the ten-year-old mind, and inasmuch as I was just ten when I first met them I became a devoted reader.

I remember one gripping little story produced by some company that sold baking powder. It showed various scenes in the life of a Mr. Brown. He was grumpy, moody, verging on failure in business, and there were pictures showing him sitting at his desk staring at nothing; obviously a man who was rapidly going down the drain. And it developed, before too long, that his loving wife was entirely responsible. She was using the wrong kind of baking powder; her biscuits were leaden or soggy, her pancakes were even worse, her cake was all but inedible, and with the best wishes in the world she was slowly poisoning her good husband.

Fortunately, before it was too late, someone introduced her to Our Sponsor's baking powder. (It either had cream of tartar, or it did not. I cannot remember which, but whichever it was, that was the key.) This made all the difference. Mr. Brown perked up no end, became happy and cheerful, kind to his family, and a jewel in the eyes of his boss. I was totally converted, and begged my mother before it was too late to switch to the right kind of baking powder. It turned out that she was dedicated to the other kind and she refused to change, pointing out that people who ate her bread, biscuits, pancakes, and so on were well and happy. So much for that. . . .

The best story of all came in a pamphlet advertising an automobile. This, I remember, was in the early days when the auto industry was no older than I was, and not much clearer in its mind about where it was going; and the auto promoted by this fable was of a hopelessly obsolete type that I can only call a motorized buggy. It looked exactly like a high-wheeled, hard-rubber-tired buggy except that it had no horse. The one-lunged motor was under the seat, the driver steered with a tiller, and even in those innocent days the type clearly was on its way out. But the advertising man had devised a most fascinating story.

The hero was a young man with his way to make; the heroine was the daughter of the local magnate, who refused to approve this romance because he wanted his daughter to marry a man who had made a lot of money. Foiled, the young couple planned to elope. Late one night, the hero drove his car—and the essential point is that his car was one of these high-wheeled buggies, which he had bought partly because it was cheaper than conventional autos and partly because, being very bright, he sensed that it had great virtues.

Anyway, the girl met him and they drove away, heading for the county seat, where they could get a license, a justice of the peace, and entrance to the blessed circle of the duly wed. The rich father had his chauffeur wheel out an expensive touring car from the family stables and set off in pursuit, vowing that he would intercept the errant couple before they got to the county seat. He knew he could do it, because he had a 45-horsepower car, whereas the elopers were riding in a queer thing with hardly any horsepower at all.

Alas, it was raining. This was before the days of paved roads, and the highway quickly turned to what the author (a ready man with an apt phrase) termed "a sea of mud." And behold—the one-lunger with high wheels straddled its way through the mud and reached its goal, while Papa's costly car bogged down and had to be towed home by horses. Young love triumphed; furthermore, after the marriage, the rich man concluded that this son-in-law must be worthy after all—he owned a car that did not get stuck in the mud—and so everybody was reconciled and the young man wound up as president of Papa's company.

This was convincing. The only trouble was that by the time I was in a position to buy an automobile the high-wheeled-buggy types were no longer being made.

AMERICAN CHARACTERS
JOHN McLOUGHLIN

The glowering presence on the left was manifestly a leader of men, accustomed to giving orders and having them obeyed—instantly. Canadian-born, he parlayed a career as director of British fur trading in the American Northwest into a place of importance in the history of the United States. He died a citizen of this country; his statue graces the South Small Rotunda of the nation's Capitol; and he is known today as "the father of Oregon." His name was John McLoughlin—*Doctor* John McLoughlin, as he would have insisted.

He was born in 1784, on a farm on the lower St. Lawrence River. An apprenticeship to a Quebec physician led to employment at nineteen as an assistant surgeon at Fort William, the North West Company's fur-gathering post on the shore of Lake Superior. He remained proud of the title of physician for the rest of his life, but in truth he was a good deal more successful as a trader. The Indians dealt readily with him, impressed by his quick mastery of their languages and by his enormous physical stature—his massive frame towered six feet four inches in a land where most tribesmen were comparatively short.

In 1814 he became a partner in the North West Company, then engaged in bloody competition with the Hudson's Bay Company. Appalled by the violent struggle—and by the dwindling profits accompanying it—McLoughlin took part in negotiations that led to an amalgamation of the two rivals. The giant doctor was then named one of the twenty-five Chief Factors, or district managers, of the continent-wide Hudson's Bay Company monopoly that resulted, and he was placed in charge of the Columbia Department. Thereafter, McLoughlin ruled some 600,000 square miles stretching from Spanish California to Russian Alaska, with twenty-two posts manned by about 460 employees. From his headquarters at Fort Vancouver on the north bank of the Columbia River near present-day Portland, Oregon, he supervised land and marine trade with the Indians of the entire Northwest; inaugurated commerce in salmon and timber with California and Hawaii; and, after 1839, supplied Russian Alaska with produce. And he managed all this under considerable pressure: no boundary yet separated British and American possessions west of the Rockies; under joint-occupancy agreements, Americans were entitled to equal rights of trade and commerce throughout the Northwest, but any sizable incursion of Yankees would necessarily jeopardize his domain.

In spite of this, he ruled like a not-always-benevolent dictator. The officers' mess gleamed with fine china and silver, and visitors at his table agreed that McLoughlin presided graciously, was a scintillating conversationalist, and could be grandly generous. But he also had a frantic temper. He quarreled so intemperately with one friend that the offended man, who was ill, left Fort Vancouver during a storm and died of exposure. When the fort's chaplain cast slurs upon McLoughlin's half-Indian wife, the outraged doctor caned the smaller man.

He seemed temperamentally unable to brook any interference with his policies—even from his superior, Sir George Simpson, with whom he bickered almost constantly. Animosity turned to rage when Simpson ordered that the marine operations of the Columbia Department be altered; McLoughlin objected with such monumental lack of tact that the two men never spoke to each other again, though the doctor retained his position.

During these altercations the influx of American settlers in the Oregon country grew steadily. For years, McLoughlin's trappers and traders had turned back would-be American competitors, but he had greeted some emigrants, especially Protestant missionaries, with more warmth than the company thought wise. The forebodings of the doctor's superiors proved sound. Glowing letters sent home by the missionaries helped quicken American migration. In 1843 McLoughlin sold—on credit—$31,000 worth of supplies to scores of destitute arrivals who had crossed the continent on the Oregon Trail. His motives were at once humane and practical, for this was a period of intense anti-British feeling in the United States, and the pioneers might have pillaged Fort Vancouver rather than starve. But from London the debts, most of them never repaid, looked like more mistaken generosity.

Finally there were the mills at Willamette Falls. Simpson and McLoughlin had long contemplated developing the water power there but had done little until American settlers started eyeing the site. McLoughlin then filed a claim, platted what he called Oregon City, and began using company funds to build saw and grist mills. Because he foresaw that the region would become American when the boundary problem was settled (as it was in 1846), and because foreign corporations could not file on land claims within the United States, he declared the mills his and sent to the company personal checks covering all costs. Simpson—doubtless with relief—accepted the payment, knowing that McLoughlin would have to resign in order to manage the property.

McLoughlin did resign, and during the California gold rush built up a thriving commerce of his own. But he remained a storm center. He tried to protect his claims by applying for U.S. citizenship when Oregon Territory was organized in 1849, but political opportunists insisted that he was a front for a foreign monopoly, and slipped a special clause depriving him of his holdings into a homestead bill passed by Congress in September, 1850.

Because of protests by many of the people he had befriended, he was never actually dispossessed. But his monumental pride had been shattered by both the nations to which he had given allegiance, and he died broken-hearted on September 3, 1857.

Five years later his claims were restored to his heirs, and in 1953 the state of Oregon unveiled a statue of him in the National Capitol—one of the two men chosen to represent the state in an august, if silent, collection of American notables. With a compassion born of hindsight, Oregon had decided to remember the good he had done and let his mistakes be interred with his gigantic bones.

by David Lavender

The Businessman and the Government

Corruption, Yesterday and Today

In this savage *1871* caricature of *Boss Tweed,* Tammany Hall's monumentally venal chieftain, Thomas Nast created a memorable symbol of the close, sometimes corrupt, partnership between American businessmen and politicians.
Harper's Weekly, OCTOBER 21, 1871

The recent spate of revelations of bribery by American corporations of government officials, domestic and foreign, has left many with a sense that the business ethics of the nation are going to hell in a handbasket. And, to be sure, the scandal—involving as it does up to now more than two hundred corporations, including many of the largest and most respected—is alarmingly and unprecedentedly pervasive; in the past, with only a few exceptions, public scandals concerning improper business influence on government have tended to focus on a single corporation and a few government officials. Sweeping moral judgments on the new state of affairs have been made of late by congressmen, journalists, and business executives not accused, and these have served the purpose that such judgments always serve—to gratify the moral sense of everyone except the judged. Now that almost everyone is feeling better, it may be well to seek the more complicated truth of the matter.

Attitudes toward business ethics in the United States move in self-generating cycles; there exists no moral equivalent of the Federal Reserve Board to smooth the cycles out, and until a way is found to fine-tune morality through legislation, no such equivalent can be created. In boom times (most recently, the late 1960's) we tend to take our profits, and avert our eyes from the possibly dismaying spectacle of how they were obtained. Come leaner years, we or our government seek scapegoats; the ethical horrors of the boom years are unveiled and paraded before us, the parade being made less frightening and more delicious by the constantly emphasized fact that it all took place in the past. Reform legislation is passed, locking the door against the fled thieves; prosperity gradually returns; new thieves with new techniques begin to operate unnoticed; and so on. And, in spite of what we may think, this cycle from public apathy to public indignation and back again takes place within a business-government climate that has been remarkably tolerant of a degree of corruption right from the start.

The first British company to colonize America, the Virginia Company, created in 1606 by royal charter, was a for-profit corporation; thus the association of government with profit in the New World stems from the first Anglo-Saxon settlement. It is little wonder that one of the early deputy governors, Samuel Argall—coming as he did from the England of James I, where government officials routinely reckoned their positions as worth so much a year in gifts and fees—exacted tribute for his personal benefit from tobacco and sassafras traders during his brief term of office, was able to maintain a sumptuous estate outside Jamestown forthrightly named "Argall's Guifte," and departed in 1619 several thousand pounds richer than when he had come two years earlier.

Graft was common in the American colonies over the succeeding century and a half. Well it might have been. British government for profit, and the colonial businessman's concomitant conclusion that his dealings with government were essentially those of one trader-for-profit with another, continued to be the rule; the nature of government income merely changed from direct tribute exacted by governors to arbitrary taxes collected by the Crown. From the colonial businessman's point of view, this change was a net loss; now, instead of paying bribes for which he got value in return, he was forced to pay taxes for which he could expect, and usually got, nothing. Then as now, the fate of the extortioner who does not deliver on his bargain was usually violence, and so it was in this case. Looked at one way, the American Revolution was the punishment imposed on a welsher.

Nor did the domestic customs of the mother country in the decade of the Revolution provide useful ethical instruction. Many British voters of the time habitually sold their votes to the highest bidder. In October, 1774, Benjamin Franklin wrote home from England—with sardonic exaggeration, to be sure—"If America would save for 3 or 4 Years the Money she spends in Fashions & Fineries & Fopperies of this Country, she might buy the whole Parliament, Minister and all." (A few years later, in the XYZ Affair, the newborn nation would get a sampling of political ethics in another foreign nation when three agents of Talleyrand, the French foreign minister, suggested to American representatives that the United States make amends for President Adams' "insults" to the French government with a loan to France of $10 million and a bribe to Talleyrand of $240,000.)

The financing of the American Revolution was solidly based on conflicts of interest exuberantly welcomed by a penniless government. Robert Morris, generally considered the financier of the Revolution, profit-

by John Brooks

"... *a cynical commentator has concluded that in fact the Revolution financed [Robert] Morris.*"
AMERICAN HERITAGE COLLECTION

ed so hugely from government contracts, many of them obtained while he himself was serving as Superintendent of Finances, that he emerged as the richest man in America; a cynical commentator has concluded that in fact the Revolution financed Morris. (Later, Morris' speculations went sour and he landed in debtors' prison.) Morris' philosophical approach to matters of business ethics is suggested by a favorite language usage of his. In his correspondence he often referred to his "integrity." Close examination of the context makes clear that what he meant by the word was his commercial credit.

Morris' younger friend and protégé, Alexander Hamilton, the authentic financial genius among the Founding Fathers, showed repeatedly that he had no qualms about institutionalizing conflict of interest, so long as he personally trusted the people he was dealing with; for example, during the money panic of 1792, when Hamilton was Secretary of the Treasury, he wrote to his old friend the cashier of the Bank of New York, of which he had been cofounder and a charter director, "If you are pressed, whatever support may be in my power shall be afforded. I consider the public interest as materially involved in a valuable institution like yours." He might, after all, have written "like mine." The previous year, according to Thomas Jefferson's later recollection, Hamilton at a private meeting with Jefferson and John Adams had seemed to come out in favor of a little graft as grease for the wheels of government when he expressed the view that the British system, "in its present form, *with* corruption and inequality," was "the most perfect that had ever existed."

It is important to note that bribery of government by business was not a feature of Revolutionary days. With a government so desperate for money that it had no choice but to plead for the cooperation of wealthy citizens, there was no need for businessmen to seek favors from government. Bribery is a function of the separation of government and business. Hamilton, indeed, as Samuel Eliot Morison points out, "set standards of honesty... that were invaluable for a people with somewhat loose financial conceptions." Still, Hamilton's advice to Morris as a government official was clear enough: "Make it the *immediate* interest of the moneyed men to cooperate with the government." That is, make it quickly profitable for them to do so. David Loth has written that Hamilton used graft "from a sense of duty." It would be more temperate to say that he used conflict of interest, but the point is unmistakable.

The moment that government and free enterprise were formally placed at arm's length by the Constitution, attempts at bribery began. It is hardly surprising that some of the attempts were successful. From the start, many congressmen regarded a measure of graft as their right and privilege. In the very first Congress in 1789, Delaware's representative, John Vining, was widely reported to have accepted a large bribe to cast the deciding vote on Hamilton's plan to fund the national debt. Senator William Maclay of Pennsylvania doubted the report, but the grounds on which he did so are hardly reassuring as to either Vining or the ethical climate in Congress. Vining's vote, the senator thought, could have been bought for one tenth of the sum reported to have been paid; the money could not have been a bribe, because surely nobody would have been such a fool as to pay so much.

In the 1790's, Jefferson was accused of gross and defamatory exaggeration when he said that most of the Senate and a large minority of the House were engaged in speculations in depreciated Continental scrip that Congress at its pleasure could cause the Treasury to redeem at par value; his figures were later confirmed by the Treasury itself. In the early years of the new century, aspiring bankers assumed that if they wanted charters, they had to buy them from the state legislature. The price for an individual vote sometimes ran as high as $5,000, the equivalent of more than five times that much now. At the federal level, the controversial Second Bank of the United States would probably not have flourished as long as it did (1816–36) but for its complaisant and intelligent habit of making unsecured loans to members of Congress, among them Henry Clay and Daniel Webster. Nicholas Biddle, head of the bank, who claimed that his power rivaled that of the President, on one occasion handed Webster $10,000 immediately after he had made a speech in favor of the bank. Webster is known to have been otherwise on the take from business interests, but we must not think too badly of him; so were many of his congressional

68

colleagues, and his shortcomings in that regard stand out only because of his unquestioned eminence as a statesman. He was following the custom of the country—a justification that echoes through the annals of American business bribery right down to the present.

In the middle 1840's, persons wishing to have the United States take over Texas' debt as part of the annexation process encouraged Congress to see the merit of such an action by distributing extensive amounts of Texas scrip and bonds to its members. The scrip and bonds would be virtually worthless unless Congress voted the U.S. takeover—which it did, to the extent of $10 million. Alleged congressional corruption by lobbyists for business interests was the subject of a flurry of suggestive, though inconclusive, investigations during the 1850's. First, the House looked into—but perhaps not far enough into—the attempted bribery of members by a lobbyist for Massachusetts manufacturers with $58,000 to dispense for a favorable tariff bill. Nothing came of this investigation. Not long afterward, in 1856, the *New York Times* Washington correspondent charged in print that "a corrupt organization of Congressmen and lobby-agents" was at large in the Capital. When the *Times* man refused to testify under oath on the matter, he was arrested and detained. Still later in the decade, the House investigated the lobbying activities of the Pacific Steamship Company, which had spent $800,000 to win a government subsidy. Nobody ever found out who got the money, but as a contemporary put the matter, "It will be a cold day in Washington when $800,000 is spent to influence legislation and some members of Congress do not get a large share of it." The *Times* man's "organization" was never identified, either; but doubtless one of its principal lights was Edward Pendleton, king of Washington lobbyists of the time, who owned an elegant gambling house on Pennsylvania Avenue. It was called formally "the Palace of Fortune," and informally "the Hall of the Bleeding Heart" by congressmen whom Pendleton affably allowed to win or favored with loans when he needed their votes. This relatively subtle form of bribery persisted in Washington until as late as the Harding administration.

After the Civil War, in which the banker Jay Cooke played a role some-

Nicholas Biddle, head of the Second Bank of the United States, gave "unsecured loans to members of Congress."
CULVER

what analogous to that of Robert Morris in the Revolution, came the golden age of graft, or, conversely, the dark age of American business-and-government ethics. Business, led by the railroads and subsequently the iron and steel industry, was becoming monstrously large, and its inclination to run roughshod over any obstacle in its way, government included, was supported by a newly conceived philosophy—Social Darwinism, the application to business affairs of Charles Darwin's theory that man has evolved to his present state through the survival of the fittest.

This era in business-government relations was ushered in, and to some extent exemplified, by the Crédit Mobilier scandal, in which a few inner stockholders of the newly organized and government-backed Union Pacific Railroad took over a Pennsylvania holding company, Crédit Mobilier of America, and used it to make exorbitant contracts with themselves to build the railroad, and thereby pocketed profits running into many millions of dollars, much of it coming from the federal treasury. The process of forestalling investigation or interference by Congress or the executive branch involved some outright bribes of government officials by the conspir-

ators, and many quasi bribes in the form of offerings of Crédit Mobilier stock to congressmen at half its market value. The affair derived a comic twist from the fact that Oakes Ames, a principal in Crédit Mobilier, was himself serving at the time as a congressman from Massachusetts. To offer his hush money he needed only speak in a congressional neighbor's ear, or at most lean across the aisle.

Indeed, comedy became a hallmark of business-government dealings in this era. The "Erie war" of 1866–68, in which "Commodore" Cornelius Vanderbilt was pitted against the unholy trinity of Daniel Drew, Jay Gould, and James Fisk, was at one stage to all intents a contest to buy injunctions from judges kept in comfort by the competing forces; as for legislators, at one point in the war Gould went to Albany, the state capital, on a secret mission, carrying with him a valise containing $500,000 in cash, and subsequently left with an empty valise. It has even been alleged that on some occasions sessions of the New York State supreme court were held informally, and no doubt conveniently, in the rooms of Fisk's mistress, Josie Mansfield. Over a period of many years the Vanderbilt interests openly maintained a captive legislator,

69

Famed Massachusetts senator Daniel Webster was known "to have been . . . on the take from business interests."
APPLETON'S CYCLOPAEDIA OF AMERICAN BIOGRAPHY, 1889

Chauncey Depew, first in the Albany legislature and later in the U.S. Senate; the Commodore's daughter-in-law refused to sit at table with Depew on grounds that his status was equivalent to that of family butler.

General cynicism, combined with the shaky sanction of Social Darwinism, had reduced, or elevated, bribery and corruption to the role of low-brow public entertainment. It was the relished, and protected, pornography of the age. The business leader most forthright on the subject, in word as well as in deed, was the railroad man Collis P. Huntington. In 1877 he explained his philosophy of bribery in a letter to a colleague, as follows: "If you have to pay money to have the right thing done, it is only just and fair to do it. . . . If a man has the power to do great evil and won't do right unless he is bribed to do it . . . it is a man's duty to go up and bribe the judge." This man of duty reported on another occasion, "I keep on *high ground*, so that we cannot be hurt by any investigation." He was also careful to insure, when possible, that the recipients of his bribes did not share the high ground; he always tried to get signed documentary evidence of the transaction, so that the bribed officials were "ever afterward my slaves." At one point in the 1870's, Huntington complained with bitter indignation that competitive bribers were causing such inflation in the corruption market as threatened to ruin him. "To fix things" now cost $200,000 to $500,000 per session of Congress: "I am fearful this damnation Congress will kill me."

This parody marketplace, with government favors all but quoted by high, low, and closing prices in the newspapers, perhaps represents the epitome of business-government ethics in the age of the robber barons. But it should be noted that by no means all businessmen even in those times played such games, and that few played them with such a lofty sense of mission as Huntington seems to have done. As Richard Huber has perceptively pointed out, Social Darwinism was too strong for the stomachs of many piously reared men of affairs; in many cases, it seems to have been imposed on them by those sophisticated men of the establishment, their lawyers. Businessmen, Huber says, "claimed that the justification for wealth was *not* climbing over the fallen bodies of others, but struggling against the evil in oneself and then going on to some kind of moral triumph. They rested their case on the Bible . . . not on the *Origin of Species*." Their roots in evangelical Christianity led to an intense ambivalence about success and the methods that brought it; this ambivalence is explicit in the writings of Andrew Carnegie, and again, interestingly enough, in the recent utterances of Bob R. Dorsey, who was deposed as chairman of Gulf Oil in 1976 for participation in corporate bribery.

It may be instructive, before leaving the post-Civil War period, to look briefly at an instance when attempted corruption failed, and to note why. In 1883 a group of Southern businessmen, political figures, and Confederate war heroes organized a company called Pan Electric, with the intention of overthrowing the Bell telephone patents and thus keeping the profits of Southern telephone service out of the hands of the Bell company Yankees. In 1885, Pan Electric had the good luck to have one of its insiders and large stockholders, Augustus H. Garland of Arkansas, named attorney general of the United States by the newly elected President, Grover Cleveland. Garland promptly used his office to further his and his colleagues' interests by bringing federal suit to annul the Bell patents. But the Marines arrived in the nick of time, in the person of William Hathaway Forbes, president of the Bell company in Boston, who talked to Cleveland and persuaded him to force Garland to drop his suit (though not to leave office). Government dishonesty in the interest of one business had been stopped in its tracks—by the *force majeure* of a larger business with a contrary interest.

The situation does not appear to have greatly improved as the twentieth century approached. In 1891 Andrew Carnegie's man, that engaging scamp Charles M. Schwab, may have inaugurated the American business custom of sealing overseas deals with ad-hoc gifts when he pressed a $200,000 necklace on the mistress of Czar Alexander's nephew—just before Bethlehem Steel got the rails contract for the huge Trans-Siberian Railroad. In 1899, toward the end of a five-year period during which were created more than five thousand business trusts covering practically every line of productive activity, the sugar baron Henry O. Havemeyer, king of one of the leading trusts, remarked, "Business is not a philanthropy. . . . I do not care two cents for your ethics. I don't

70

know enough of them to apply them." The important point, perhaps, is that Havemeyer's turn-of-the-century interlocutor *did* have a sense of business ethics, and cared enough to ask Havemeyer about his. Reform was in the air at last.

The new century, however one may rate businessmen's ethical performance in it, brought a huge increase in public and government concern on the subject. Federal regulation and control of business had begun formally, though not at first effectively, with the Interstate Commerce Act of 1887 and the Sherman Antitrust Act of 1890. Now two great reform waves, the Progressive movement of roughly 1902-12 and the New Deal of 1933-40, brought to Washington hordes of reformers burning to set businessmen and legislators alike on the path of righteousness. It was encouraging news for them when Henry Clay Frick, after he had helped finance Theodore Roosevelt's 1904 presidential campaign, complained with evident chagrin, "We got nothing for our money." Still, there was plenty of reforming to be done. David Graham Phillips' *The Treason of the Senate,* the appearance of which in 1907 in Hearst's *Cosmopolitan* magazine gave rise to Roosevelt's popularization of the term "muckraker," depicted the Senate as little more than a paid department of the trusts, and named specific senators as "perjurers" and "thieves"—charges that gave rise to no libel suits and were never effectively refuted. In 1907 Congress at last passed a law making illegal all political contributions by corporations (as distinguished from individuals) to candidates for federal office.

Like so many other pieces of early reform legislation—including notably the Sherman Act—this one was for years honored chiefly in the breach. Nevertheless, the Progressive era certainly left business bribers and federal bribe-takers somewhat chastened. The people had shown that they cared; what had been conceived as comedy became moral drama, and the concept of public office as a public trust subject to sanctions other than the trustees' own consciences was at last formally written down. But both sides needed only wait for the next turn of the cycle. The Teapot Dome affair during the inept Harding administration after the First World War, in which Secretary of the Interior Albert B. Fall accepted bribes

"It is [sometimes] a man's duty," said railroad mogul Collis P. Huntington, *"to go up and bribe the judge."*
CULVER

from oilmen in exchange for secretly granted leases to government oil reserves in Wyoming and California, gave rise to a great public outcry, and Fall went to jail. Essentially, it was Crédit Mobilier replayed. During the middle 1920's, business-government relations looked back even further. With Calvin Coolidge in the White House and the Pittsburgh multimillionaire Andrew W. Mellon as head of the Treasury, government's attitude toward business was like that of a believer more Catholic than the Pope. Mellon represented the concept, later widely extended, of the public servant thought to be free of temptation because he was so rich. In fact, bribes were unnecessary anyhow; Mellon out of conviction not only met but tried to anticipate every need of business. The country was back to the prebribery alliance of business and government in the state-capitalism days of Hamilton.

The flood of reform legislation passed during the New Deal years was directed chiefly at establishing more fairness in business relations with labor and the consumer, rather than in fighting business-government corruption or collusion. Indeed, those years mark a major turning point in the financial relations between those two entities, and not necessarily a healthy one. For the first time in history, the federal government in peacetime became a financial giant with vast sums to dispense. Total federal government expenditures came to $4.66 billion in 1932; by 1940 they had climbed to $9 billion and by 1941 to $13 billion. During World War II, military production needs sent the figure soaring to about $100 billion per year; and in the postwar years, to the surprise of most economists, federal spending remained at previously unheard-of peacetime figures: in the first five postwar years it averaged $42 billion, almost ten times the 1932 figure. One result of the creation of this enormous pork barrel was that the direction of flow of corrupt money was largely reversed; the post World War II era was the first peacetime period when government had more financial favors to confer on business than vice versa. (Crédit Mobilier and Teapot Dome had both been made possible by government acts under war conditions.)

The logical new form of bribery was, of course, the kickback for a government contract award, rather than the direct bribe for a favorable legislative climate. It appears that the vast waste of government funds

71

Albert B. Fall, Warren Harding's Secretary of the Interior, "accepted bribes from oilmen... and went to jail."
U.P.I.

during the war years resulted more from inefficiency and ineptitude than from bribery. The government had spent $5.8 billion by the end of 1943 in the settlement of *cancelled* contracts alone. Blair Bolles tells us of one lucky contractor who first valued his inventory at $1.068 million, then sold it to the government for $2.137 million, and shortly thereafter, the government having found the goods unsuitable for its purposes, bought it back for $339,000; yet no bribes had changed hands. The wartime atmosphere, with a few variations, carried over into the postwar years. The mink coats and deep freezers of Harry Truman's time, and the Oriental rugs of Dwight Eisenhower's, were penny-ante stuff; particularly in the years of Truman, the coin of influence on government was usually not cash but cronyism. In retrospect, the years 1945–60 appear as a silver, if not a golden, age in business-government ethics. Handing out public money to old pals for the sake of friendship, all moral and legal authorities agree, is less sinful than handing it out in exchange for bribes from strangers. The advantage to the citizenry is, however, less clear.

As we have recently learned, it was in the 1960's that, with Uncle Sam's role as angel to business sharply curtailed by other commitments, bribery by business to influence legislation got a new lease on life. Gulf Oil inaugurated its now-famous Bahamas slush fund in 1960; by that July the first $150,000 had been drawn on it and duly delivered to deserving legislators. Within a few years, if we may believe Gulf's chief Washington lobbyist at the time, illegal payments had been made, either directly or via their staffs, to forty-five members of Congress, including various key men on key committees and a future President of the United States, Lyndon B. Johnson. Many other corporations have confessed that, particularly late in the decade, they indulged in similar activities. Meanwhile, as the overseas operations of large American corporations expanded at an unprecedented rate, bribery of foreign officials and their governments not only made a piker of Charles Schwab but seems to have become the rule rather than the exception. Two forces were behind this sinister second blooming of unethical business conduct at home and abroad: the fact that, beyond question, in many of the foreign countries where American corporations now operated for the first time on a large scale, bribes were the accepted if not the required custom; and on the domestic front, the accession to power in 1969 of an administration of such ruthlessness and political cynicism that even the best-intentioned business enterprises were often made to feel that it was a case of pay tribute or die. It would be cynicism of another sort to suggest that a third force behind the bribery revival was that of time-honored American tradition.

The attitude of leading businessmen toward ethical questions in the middle 1970's—a time of reformism in Washington and, one might hope, penitence in corporate boardrooms—must give the righteous pause. In a report on a series of meetings held in 1974–75, the members of the Conference Board, the most respected of national organizations of leading executives, expressed their views forthrightly, if in almost every case anonymously. The executives' prevailing attitude seemed to hold paranoia and smugness in delicate balance. "The harassment of the businessman by the government bureaucracy stamps out productivity," said one. The press and television, many participants felt, are another source of harassment: "The media are destructive and misinformed." "The press is forever at war with the creative minds of free men." Certainly there was some truth in these strictures; but how easy is it to agree with the view of one participant, echoed by others, that "Deep down in their hearts most people trust us [corporations] more than they do any other institution"? Such a statement, in the present context, seems to suggest either a blindfolded eye or an underdeveloped brain. The bribery scandals per se were tactfully left all but unmentioned in the discussions, but nevertheless were a tacit presence; the implied attitude of the participants toward them was reflected in repeated identification of "poor communications" as the root cause of the public's current low estimate of business. Corporations, the Conference Board consensus went, are already socially responsible, and need not be prodded to become more so; their shortcoming has been in too modestly mumbling the recital of their virtues. Yet the real communications problem, at least over the years since 1973, seems more likely to have been that the corporations have communicated all too well.

At the same time, the Conference Board report and other recent utterances of business leaders make clear that their sense of ethical responsibility has changed subtly over the years, and for the better. The very concept of the social responsibility of corporations dates only from the turn of the century, and perhaps it needs more than three quarters of a century to mature. Compare, for example, Collis P. Huntington a century ago ("It is a man's duty to go up and bribe the judge") or Havemeyer a generation later ("I do not care two cents for your ethics") with William K. Whiteford, then chairman of Gulf Oil, writing in the early 1960's to an officer of the Bahamas bank that was handling Gulf's slush fund: ". . . The next time I have to make a confidential arrangement to secure political funds, I can put the blame on the Bank should that great institution . . . fail to protect my anonymity." Whiteford was presenting the precise truth as if it were a flight of fancy—that is, he was employing that great resource of the modern American businessman treading on thin ice, jocularity. A child, or a businessman, who uses uneasy jokes as a cover is thereby admitting to a sense of guilt; Huntington would never have dreamed of doing that. Or listen to Daniel J. Haughton, former chairman of the Lockheed Corporation, which had paid millions of dollars in bribes in a variety of foreign countries. Testifying before a Senate subcommittee in 1975, Haughton said of such bribery, "I am not arguing that it is a good practice. . . . I am saying unless everybody plays by the same rules, if you are going to win it is necessary. . . . In doing business abroad, anyway up to now, you have to take into consideration the customs of the countries and the customers where you are doing business." The reader will observe that this is *almost* saying, as Huntington said, that sometimes a person "won't do right unless he is bribed"—almost, but not quite.

"Businessmen have a different set of delusions from politicians," John Maynard Keynes advised President Roosevelt in 1937. ". . . You could do anything you like with them, if you would treat them not as wolves or tigers, but as domestic animals." Or as Dr. Johnson put the matter, "There are few ways in which a man can be more innocently employed than making money." On the whole, domestic animals innocently employed seems an inadequate metaphor for Robert Morris, Nicholas Biddle, Collis P. Huntington, or Daniel Haughton.

Present-day Americans have a widespread and often-noted tendency to idealize the national past. That such a view extends to the ethical conduct of businessmen and legislators is indicated by the shock and disbelief that have greeted the recent revelations of corporate misconduct. Why this tendency to nostalgia should exist is a subject for psychologists and anthropologists; surely it is related to the golden-age myths that are part of the folklore of many cultures, among them those of Greece, India, China, Persia, and Babylonia, and that have a Judeo-Christian counterpart in the story of the lost Eden. However, in the case at hand, myth it is. If we believe that American businessmen and legislators now are less ethical than they used to be, we are wrong; if anything, they are more so. To a quite limited extent, the United States has succeeded in legislating morality.

Are we to conclude, then, that the familiar and cherished American folk hero, the high-minded businessman-gentleman of the past, never really existed and is himself a figure of myth? To do so would be rash. The evidence, impressive as it is, deals exclusively with the conduct of big businessmen operating in big cities. The factual annals of the small-scale, small-town businessman are scanty; he is chronicled chiefly in fiction, where he appeared regularly as a person of integrity until Sinclair Lewis with Babbitt made him a figure of fun and William Faulkner with the Snopes family made him a . . . Snopes. Still cherished even by some modern leftists as a sort of Dead Father, the small businessman as revered gentleman survives as a memory rather than a myth.

As for the big-business bribery revelations, the fact that they follow in a tradition is, I believe, no reason not to be horrified by them. It is, however, reason not to be shocked by them. It is also reason for us to adopt, if we can, a more mature attitude toward a national problem: to be less naïvely condoning of corruption in good times and less naïvely condemning in bad; and, perhaps above all, to put in the context of past ethical standards at home the argument that American business bribes abroad are made necessary by low ethical standards among the backward natives.

John Brooks often writes on business history. Among his books is Once in Golconda: A True Drama of Wall Street 1920–1938 *(Harper & Row, 1969).*

". . . if you are going to win," said Daniel J. Haughton, former Lockheed chairman, "[bribery] is necessary."
WIDE WORLD

In the month of February, 1846, when conditions for travel were as unpropitious as possible, the Mormons began moving out of their newly built city of Nauvoo, Illinois, in order to cross the ice-strewn Mississippi, on the first leg of a long and uncertain journey. A forced abandoning of barely completed homes, this time with the loss of much property and the necessity for travel in the dead of winter, was no new experience for the adherents of the Church of Jesus Christ of Latter-day Saints. Twice before, in Ohio and Missouri, the violence of their non-Mormon neighbors had forced the "Saints" to give up newly established colonies, but Nauvoo was the worst disaster yet, for in 1844 an Illinois lynching mob had murdered Joseph Smith, founder of the Mormon Church, the man who claimed to have talked with God and angels, the man who claimed to have found and translated the golden tablets on which the Book of Mormon was engraved, the man who had directed—some would say dictated—every social, economic, political, and religious aspect of Mormon daily life.

As her family's laden wagons struggled down to the shore of the icebound Mississippi, the awesome dangers of the venture were all too clear to Sarah D. Rich, who later

THE MORMONS

From Poverty and Persecution to Prosperity and Power

by Rodman W. Paul

recorded her emotions in an appealingly misspelled manuscript:

"To start out on such a jeorney in the winter as it ware and in our state of poverty it would seam like walking into the jaws of death. But we had faith in our heavenly father and we put our trust in him, feeling that we ware his chosen people and had imbraced his gospel and insted of sorrow we felt to rejoice that the day of deliverence had come."

A "chosen people," the elect of God, the only true believers—such phrases characterized the Mormons as they saw themselves. The confident faith that inspired such thinking was at once a force that held the Mormons together and an irritant that antagonized those who were not Mormons ("Gentiles," as the Saints called them). Despite, or perhaps because of, the Mormons' remarkable success in creating a vigorously independent and thriving city at Nauvoo, the assaults of the Gentiles had made life in Illinois too dangerous and costly to be endured. Smith's principal successor, Brigham Young, had taken the lead in determining that the Mormons must begin a massive folk migration that would carry them far beyond contact with non-Mormons. The plan finally decided upon was to cross the vast emptiness of the Great Plains to some as yet uncertain point just beyond the Rockies. It would be a huge undertaking that would require several years, for ultimately over fifteen thousand people and whatever belongings they had salvaged in their enforced winter exodus had to be moved more than a thousand miles and resettled in a desert.

To any dispassionate observer, a folk migration begun in the worst time of year and with shortages of wagons, teams, and food must have seemed truly a case of "walking into the jaws of death," as Mrs. Rich expressed it. By all logic, this should have been the moment for Mormonism to break up. With their prophet and original organizer murdered, their homes lost, and signs of dissidence among them, the Mormons in this dreary winter of 1846 should have been ready to follow many another new sect into disintegration and ineffectuality.

But what in fact is the status of the Mormons today, more than 130 years after their trek to the land of Zion in the Salt Lake Valley of Utah? They are one of the fastest-growing and most prosperous denominations in the country. They claim nearly 2,500,000 adherents within the United States and another million overseas, and thanks to energetic proselytizing at home and abroad, their numbers increase almost daily. So does their influence. The Mormons, who were unsophisticated, poorly educated rural folk in 1846, have joined the general American trend by turning away from the countryside to dwell in suburbs and cities, and away from farming and simple crafts to the professions, commerce, finance, and industry.

Today more than half of the American Mormons live outside Utah and its immediate neighbors, and they are as likely to be found directing major businesses and real-estate operations in Los Angeles, Detroit, or New York as working in Salt Lake City. Nor do they confine themselves to private business. They have contributed senators, congressmen, governors, and presidential candidates. In local affairs they have won membership on school boards, city councils, and citizens' advisory groups. Their attitudes are precisely those one would expect of an affluent, confident middle class blessed with homes of visible comfort. While there are liberals among them, most, especially among the leaders, are political conservatives. Unlike their forefathers of three generations ago, they no longer favor social or economic experimentation, be it in town building, irrigation systems, or multiple wives. They still have a remarkable cohesiveness, but much of their force is directed inward now, toward strengthening the church by conserving its membership, rather than outward toward meeting widely felt social or economic needs.

How do we account for this extraordinary change in the Mormons' numbers, fortunes, and attitudes? Can an analysis of their history supply explanations that will satisfy Mormons and non-Mormons alike? The significance of the Saints makes an attempt well worth the effort, for in the nineteenth and early twentieth centuries the Mormons were the most important single colonizing agency in settling the huge Western region between the Rocky Mountains and the Sierra Nevada-Cascades, and today they seem on their way to becoming leaders in the nation as a whole.

The story begins with the unity that came to the Mormons as the result of sharing an unusual faith, a faith that automatically set its believers apart from the general population. Most Protestant splinter groups merely reinterpreted the accepted King James Bible and rearranged some existing pattern of church government, but Mormonism went far beyond that, for it asserted that there had been modern revelations from God to an actual, known nineteenth-century human being, Joseph Smith of western New York State.

Smith was the son of debt-ridden, ill-educated parents who had drifted out of New England to make a new (and ultimately unsuccessful) beginning at Palmyra, New York, a town situated between the head of the Finger Lakes and Lake Ontario. This was part of the "burned-over" district,

---

PRECEDING PAGE: *On July 24, 1897, the fiftieth anniversary of the Mormons' entry into Salt Lake Valley, the Mormon Temple, looming over the domed Tabernacle in Salt Lake City, was draped with one of the largest American flags in existence, one made in the Overall Works of Zion's Co-operative Mercantile Institute. Unfortunately, workmen had installed the pegs for the banner backwards. There was at that time no uniform code for the display of the flag, and the Mormons, pragmatic as always, went ahead and hung it wrong-end-to.*

SPECIAL COLLECTIONS, MARRIOTT LIBRARY, UNIVERSITY OF UTAH

so called because during Joseph Smith's youth wave after wave of emotional religious revivals—the fires of God—swept through the region.

Like his neighbors, Smith matured in an atmosphere of poverty and slight education, but he was notable for a high native intelligence. At some point in the 1820's, according to Smith's own account, an angel in "a loose robe of most exquisite whiteness" appeared in Smith's bedroom and informed him of the existence of a sacred book, the Book of Mormon, that was "written upon gold plates" and buried on a hill "convenient to the village of Manchester, Ontario County, New York." After a four-year delay during which he had to purify himself, Smith believed himself divinely commissioned to translate the text of the golden tablets from an ancient language into 275,000 words of more-or-less King James Version English. The huge manuscript was then set into print in 1830 on a local newspaper press and published as *The Book of Mormon: An Account Written by the Hand of Mormon, Upon Plates Taken from the Plates of Nephi,* by Joseph Smith, Junior, "Author and Proprietor."

Faith in the authenticity of that book was essential to membership in what officially became known as the Church of Jesus Christ of Latter-day Saints. To accept Mormonism one had to believe *literally* that an angel revealed to Smith this hitherto unknown sacred book, comparable to the Bible, and, further, that thereafter God repeatedly communicated with Joseph Smith, whose revelations of God's will were both numerous and explicit, ranging from general rules for the government of the church to highly specific instructions to named individuals. Those who were capable of literal belief in so revolutionary a set of religious assumptions inevitably set themselves apart from the skeptical or derisive majority of Americans, and thus became what the Mormons themselves called a "peculiar people." Becoming a "peculiar people" in turn led to persecution and to the martyrdom of their prophet, Joseph Smith. Paradoxically, the assaults upon them had a unifying effect: nothing so unites a group as the sense of standing together against a hostile world.

But their ability to hold together was facilitated also by something that was as unique as the modern revelation upon which the Mormon faith was founded. Joseph Smith had created the only true theocracy that America has ever seen. One dictionary defines theocracy as a "system of government by priests claiming a divine commission." In the Mormon Church, from Smith's time to the present day, there have never been professional priests. Instead, every adult white male of good character is a priest and by hard work can rise to successively higher rank and responsibility in the church's very definite hierarchy.

Brigham Young toured the frontier outposts of his empire on a regular basis. He is seen above, in high hat, seated in the middle of a splendid retinue, during one such expedition to southern Utah in 1870.
UTAH STATE HISTORICAL SOCIETY

The individual male earns his living in a regular secular job and must manage to do his own work while meeting the church's very heavy demands upon his time. The only exceptions are at the pinnacle of the Mormon hierarchy, where the sheer weight of responsibilities makes it necessary for the individual to give up his secular calling in order to devote full time to the church's demands. Save at the very top, where a "living allowance" is provided, no one gets paid for doing the church's work; on the contrary, all Mormons are expected to support this elaborate organization by paying a genuine tithe—a real 10 per cent of their income.

Women and blacks may not become priests. The women are expected to work hard as a kind of ladies' auxiliary, but they must achieve glorification and satisfaction in the church through their husbands' service to the church and through the bearing of children. Annie Clark Tanner, who was born in rural Utah in 1864 and raised as the daughter of Wife Number Two in a devout polygamous family, summed up the underlying philosophy in two sentences:

"The Priesthood is a spiritual power which purports to give man superior wisdom. Because of this superiority in power and authority, a wife was subservient to her husband." If such an attitude sounds absurd today, in the nineteenth century it was not very remote from views widely accepted among the general American population.

Before she was twenty, Annie Clark herself became Wife Number Two of a polygamous husband, thus beginning what proved to be a singularly unhappy, unstable, yet long-continued marital relationship (ten children). Her own and her mother's experiences led her to comment on the obvious connection between her church's attitude toward women and its stubborn defense of its most publicized institution, polygamy. "Polygamy," Mrs. Tanner said, "is predicated on the assumption that man is superior to woman," and that man must be given "privileged rights in domestic affairs."

The church's stand on blacks has become even more anachronistic than its attitudes toward women. Blacks are encouraged to join, but unlike other males, they must not expect to enter the priesthood. According to Mormon belief, their color means that they bear a lifelong curse as the descendants of one of the sons of Adam and Eve, Cain, who in a fit of jealousy slew his brother Abel. For this bloody deed, Cain and his descendants were cursed with black skins—the "mark of Cain." Someday, Mormon theory runs, the curse will be lifted, but until that time participation in the priesthood is forbidden to blacks, although not to some other nonwhites, such as Polynesians. For modern Mormon liberals, the church's flat prohibition—and the blunt implication of racial inferiority—has become a heavy cross.

From the beginning the Mormon Church has thus been an organization that is staffed by unpaid white male nonprofessionals, and is supported by remarkably generous giving by all loyal Mormons. The church is organized into successively higher levels of authority, beginning at the level of the local congregation, which is called a "ward" and is presided over by a layman called a "bishop," and rising up through a larger geographical entity called a "stake," above which are the central authorities of the church, who have operated out of Salt Lake City ever since the Mormons have been in Utah. Twice a year there is a huge meeting in Salt Lake City to which the faithful are earnestly urged to come. It is at those semiannual meetings that the faithful are told what their leaders have decided.

How are officials chosen for these different levels? Joseph Smith declared that his church was to be not so much a theocracy but rather what he termed a "theo-democracy." In practice this has meant that the leaders of the church select some promising Mormon for a post, and then ask the people of the particular group he will lead to ratify the choice by a show of hands in meeting. The approval so given is known as the "sustaining vote." Normally it is forthcoming, since the voting group knows that the nomination represents their leaders'

THE DOMESTIC BLISS OF BRIGHAM YOUNG

While their religion differed from orthodox Protestantism in many respects, the most "peculiar institution" of the Mormons was polygamy, which they insisted was ordained by the Scriptures. Orthodoxy disagreed, and until 1890, when the church officially renounced the practice, polygamy was a constant source of pious outrage and derision—such as in the 1877 cartoon at left, which manages to combine cruelty and prurience with a raw humor. Mark Twain was a good deal more gentle in his own remarks on the subject. He had stopped off in Salt Lake City on his way West in 1861, and in *Roughing It,* published in 1872, he fantasized about certain practical difficulties in the daily life of Brigham Young:

"None of our party got an opportunity to take dinner with Mr. Young, but a Gentile by the name of Johnson professed to have enjoyed a sociable breakfast in the Lion House. He gave a preposterous account of the 'calling of the roll,' and other preliminaries, and the carnage that ensued when the buckwheat cakes came in. But he embellished rather too much. He said that Mr. Young told him several smart sayings of certain of his 'two-year-olds,' observing with some pride that for many years he had been the heaviest contributor in that line to one of the Eastern magazines; and then he wanted to show Mr. Johnson one of the pets that had said the last good thing, but he could not find the child. He searched the faces of the children in detail, but could not decide which one it was. Finally he gave it up....

" 'I thought I would know the little cub again but I don't.'

"Mr. Johnson said further, that Mr. Young observed that life was a sad, sad thing—'because the joy of every new marriage a man contracted was so apt to be blighted by the inopportune funeral of a less recent bride.' And Mr. Johnson said that while he and Mr. Young were pleasantly conversing in private, one of the Mrs. Youngs came in and demanded a breast-pin,

wishes and, as Mrs. Tanner remarked, "obedience was the basis of our religion." From Joseph Smith's time to the present this elaborate church structure has provided a definite place and role for every active Mormon. The energies, the enthusiasms, and money of each member are enlisted.

The church has dominated not only the religious life of its members but also their social life, frequently their political life, and at times their economic activities. After the Mormons moved to Utah, the church created and controlled the only government Utah had until 1850. When Congress established a territorial form of government in that year, Brigham Young became the first governor, and the church remained a *de facto* force in government at all levels. Nor did the church's influence in government cease after the federal government displaced Brigham Young as territorial governor in 1857.

This theocracy could operate the more easily because from the beginning the Mormons had shown a remarkable spirit of communitarian cooperation. Because the early Mormons were too poor and too limited in education and experience to undertake big projects as individuals, they learned to work together under the leadership of their church. By pooling their labor under church direction, and employing only the simplest tools and equipment, they planned and built towns, irrigation canals, roads, and factories—without accumulating a large capital debt.

Joseph Smith initiated these arrangements and developed a cadre of effective leaders who served as his immediate subordinates. For his administrative accomplishments he deserves more credit than he has usually received. At his death in 1844 Joseph Smith was succeeded by one of the outstanding organizers of the nineteenth century, Brigham Young, who ruled the church until his own death in 1877. If the circumstances of his life had worked out differently, Brigham Young might have become a captain of industry—an Andrew Carnegie or John D. Rockefeller or perhaps a railroad builder.

Young's beginnings in rural Vermont and New York State were as humble as Joseph Smith's. He once declared that he had had only eleven days of formal schooling. Yet in adult life, when he stood at the head of the Mormon Church, he impressed his visitors. In 1860, Sir Richard Burton, the famous British world traveler, found him "at once affable and impressive, simple and courteous: his want of pretension contrasts favorably with certain pseudo-prophets that I have seen. . . . He impresses a stranger with a certain sense of power. . . . He can use all the weapons of ridicule to direful effect" and can reprimand his followers "in purposely violent language." Albert D. Richardson, the journalist, added his own evaluation in 1867:

"With an affable and dignified manner he manifests the unmistakable egotism of one having authority. In little ebullitions of earnestness he speaks right at people, using his dexter forefinger with emphasis, to point a moral. He treats the brethren with warmth, throwing his arm caressingly about them and asking carefully after the wives and babies.

"Provincialisms of his Vermont boyhood and his western manhood still cling to him. He says 'leetle,' 'beyand' and 'disremember.' An irrepressible conflict between his nominatives and verbs, crops out in expressions like 'they was.' "

This able, energetic, earthy man became the absolute ruler and the revered, genuinely loved father figure of all Mormons everywhere. He used the church hierarchy as the instrument through which he ruled, and from among the church leaders he selected the captains and lieutenants he needed to carry out his purposes. But Young himself was a master of detail who kept in touch with everything. In his letters to his sons he constantly exhorted his progeny to observe, improve, work, and be useful. He held himself to those same exacting standards. Whenever he traveled, which he did frequently, he always knew a great deal about not only each town he visited but also many of the individuals who lived there. To a hard-working rural Mormon, it meant everything that the ruler of the church knew that Sister Eliza had had an unusually hard time after the birth of her sixth child, or that Brother Isaiah had been the principal carpenter in rebuilding the local church after

---

remarking that she had found out that he had been giving a breast-pin to No. 6, and *she,* for one, did not propose to let this partiality go on without making a satisfactory amount of trouble about it. Mr. Young reminded her that there was a stranger present. Mrs. Young said that if the state of things inside the house was not agreeable to the stranger, he could find room outside. Mr. Young promised the breast-pin, and she went away. But in a minute or two another Mrs. Young came in and demanded a breast-pin. Mr. Young began a remonstrance, but Mrs. Young cut him short. She said No. 6 had got one, and No. 11 was promised one, and it was 'no use for him to try to impose on her—she hoped she knew her rights.' He gave his promise, and she went. And presently three Mrs. Youngs entered in a body and opened on their husband a tempest of tears, abuse, and entreaty. They had heard all about No. 6, No. 11, and No. 14. Three more breast-pins were promised. They were hardly gone when nine more Mrs. Youngs filed into the presence, and a new tempest burst forth and raged round about the prophet and his guest. Nine breast-pins were promised, and the weird sisters filed out again. And in came eleven more, weeping and wailing and gnashing their teeth. Eleven promised breast-pins purchased peace once more.

" 'That is a specimen,' said Mr. Young. 'You see how it is. You see what a life I lead. A man *can't* be wise all the time. . . . My friend, take an old man's advice, and *don't* encumber yourself with a large family—mind, I tell you, don't do it. In a small family, and in a small family only, you will find that comfort and that peace of mind which are the best at last of the blessings this world is able to afford us, and for the lack of which no accumulation of wealth, and no acquisition of fame, power, and greatness can ever compensate us. Take my word for it, ten or eleven wives is all you need—never go over it.' "

79

it had suffered storm damage.

His visits to local communities were rustic versions of a royal progress. All of the townsmen put on their best clothes, buildings were decorated, the street strewn with flowers, the brass band played, and the school children sang:

Come join the army, the army of our Lord,
Brigham is our leader, we'll rally at his
  word.
Sharp will be the conflict with the powers of
  sin,
But with such a leader we are sure to win.

Young could be ruthless and crude, but he had many qualities more notable than his most publicized achievement, which was the admittedly impressive catalog of his wives—ultimately he married twenty-seven women. The most reliable statisticians credit Young with fifty-six or fifty-seven children by sixteen of those wives. Even with the separate apartments that he maintained for them, Young's ability to keep so many wives from quarreling and so many children from overwhelming him would in itself prove that he must have been a remarkable, not to say masterful, diplomat.

During the thirty years between the Mormons' arrival in Utah in 1847 and 1877, Young directed the founding of 350 towns in the Southwest. A modern historian has remarked that the two most important forces in settling the intermountain West were the Union Pacific Railroad and the Mormon Church—two large, well-organized, and centrally directed institutions. In such a harsh geographic setting, the job could not possibly have been done by exclusive reliance upon the efforts of unorganized individuals.

How the process worked was illustrated by the founding of the town of Springville, southeast of Salt Lake. Although two Mormon militiamen discovered the site early in 1849, Brigham Young decreed that settlement must await the arrival of Bishop Aaron Johnson, who was to lead a wagon train across the plains to Utah during the summer of 1850. Johnson, who like so many of the early Mormons was of New England ancestry (Connecticut-born), was just the kind of proven leader to whom Brigham Young habitually turned when a difficult new task was at hand.

A Mormon since 1836, only six years after Joseph Smith had founded the denomination, Johnson had risen to successively higher responsibilities during the Mormons' town-building in Ohio, Missouri, and Illinois and during their exodus from Nauvoo. When the bearded bishop finally brought his train of 135 wagons safely to Salt Lake City, Brigham Young came to greet the newcomers and arbitrarily "cut out" the first eight wagons, announcing to their drivers that they were to go with Johnson to found Springville. From his own family Johnson, in turn, selected two of his wives and three of his sons to accompany him with this advance detachment.

The chosen site was a lovely one. Tall wild grasses covered a strip of virgin land that had the massive Wasatch Range of the Rockies at its back, and the glittering waters of Utah Lake before it, while Hobble Creek, flowing out from the mountain canyons, gave assurance of water for irrigation.

Under Johnson's leadership, the necessary tasks were quickly assigned. Some were to harvest the wild grasses with scythes; others were to take axes and teams up into the mountains to bring out logs; while still others were to lay out a fortified settlement that would cover an acre and a half, big enough to shelter both settlers and domestic livestock from the possibility of Indian attack and the certainty of winter storms. Typical of the Mormons, one of the early buildings was a schoolhouse and another a structure large enough for dances and social gatherings, and presently for amateur theatricals, for the Mormons never let their New England heritage lead them into discouraging harmless pleasures and sociability.

There were difficult early years at Springville when poor crops reduced the pioneers to eating thistle roots, pig weed, red root, and sego bulbs, but by the time Johnson died in 1877, worn out from too many years of multivarious duties, the town had long been a decided success. Johnson had been bishop, judge, brigadier general of local militia, philanthropist to all in need, and "head of all the public affairs," as his son expressed it. Family tradition has it that his children numbered fifty-five and his wives either eleven or thirteen. (A slight uncertainty, where the numbers are so high, can easily be forgiven.)

Most of the towns that Young caused to be founded were in arid regions that required irrigation systems and the careful use of limited supplies of water, timber, and good land, needs which the Mormons fulfilled in their own, almost revolutionary manner. For the United States as a whole this was an age of unrestrained laissez faire, in which the primary standard of judgment was private profit rather than community need, but the Mormons immediately placed social values ahead of individual desires. Towns were planned according to the old New England pattern: the residences and their attendant kitchen gardens were clustered in the middle of the town, so that the people would be close to neighbors, the school, and the church building, while the irrigable crop lands were out in the more open country beyond the settlement, and the pasture lands were still farther away. Water was declared by Brigham Young to be the property of *all* the people rather than private property, and was to be distributed through an irrigation system built under church leadership and by the labor of the people who would be using it. Use of the water was tied to the land that needed it and was regulated by the local people, so that water monopoly was impossible. When disputes about water arose, they were usually taken to the local bishop of the church ward for his mediation or arbitration, instead of spending time and money to file suit in the courts.

In declaring water to be the property of the whole community, and in working out this simple pattern for use, Young and his people were discarding several centuries of Anglo-American precedents developed under the common law for use in a humid climate. Elsewhere in the West a great deal of expensive litigation could have been avoided if lawyers and legislators had been more willing to throw away Blackstone's *Commentaries* and follow the example set by the unsophisticated but pragmatic Mormons.

In Brigham Young's eyes, building towns and irrigation systems was not enough. The Mormons had always wanted to make themselves economically self-sufficient, so that they would not be at the mercy of the nation's non-Mormon majority when they needed supplies. Once they had become settled in Utah and had survived the difficult first years, they began a remarkable if unsuccessful drive to create all kinds of industries and services. Factories, mills, an iron foundry, express and teamster services, local railroads, cooperative stores, woolen mills, cotton growing, and a sugar-beet industry were examples of ventures that Young persuaded the faithful to finance through drafts upon the local congregations to supply money, labor, draft animals, and raw materials. Unfortunately, these subsidized ventures were, at best, high-cost enterprises producing for a limited market, and after the transcontinental railroad was completed in 1869, cheaper, better-finished goods flooded in from the Middle West and East to wipe out such of the Mormon experiments as had not already failed of their own unsoundness.

The sum total of all these efforts suggests how and why the Mormons were able to hold together and indeed to grow steadily in numbers and resources through the difficult and crucial years of the 1850's, 1860's, and 1870's. They were united by accepting an unusual faith; they were led by a remarkable man who headed a theocracy that penetrated every aspect of daily life and could normally count upon obedient responses to its directives; and they were addicted to cooperative, communitarian ways of meeting all challenges. But in addition to these forces from within, they were strengthened in their loyalty to the church by the periodic attacks made upon them by the United States government, which in turn was responding to the hostile public opinion constantly being whipped up by reformers, newspaper editors, politicians, and women's organizations. In 1857 President James Buchanan, who was soon to vacillate over coercing the seceding Southern states, did not hesitate to send the United States Army into Utah under the command of the future Confederate general Albert Sidney Johnston to compel the Mormons to accept federal rule and federal law. Inevitably, a morbidly illogical act of retaliation took place: the "Mountain Meadows Massacre" of September, 1857, in which more than one hundred members of a Gentile emigrant train passing through Utah were slaughtered, almost certainly by Mormons in alliance with friendly Indians. This event, which Mormon historian Juanita Brooks has called "one of the most despicable mass murders of history," was an aberration, a paranoid re-

PUBLIC COMMUNICATIONS OFFICE, CHURCH OF JESUS CHRIST OF LATTER-DAY SAINTS

GRANITE IS FOREVER

The photograph above shows the entrances to one of the largest underground complexes on earth, one carved out of the solid rock of the Wasatch Range at the mouth of Cottonwood Canyon some twenty miles east of Salt Lake City. Its access tunnels are sealed by steel doors weighing nine tons each and further protected by iron gates; uniformed guards make their rounds and a closed-circuit television system monitors all movement inside. Emergency generators lie in readiness should the occasion arise, and a reserve water system containing thirty-six thousand gallons can be tapped for the use of the eighty workers who man the files and catalogues and computers that fill the tunnels and cavernous rooms. Overhead, more than seven hundred feet of granite provides a shield against natural or man-made catastrophe.

It is not a back-up facility of the Defense Department's huge NORAD bunker somewhere in the Midwest, nor is it a secret CIA operation; it is the Granite Mountain Genealogical Vault, constructed by the Church of Jesus Christ of Latter-day Saints in 1965 at a cost of more than two million dollars. It is the largest genealogical library anywhere in the world. Its more than 980,000 catalogued rolls of microfilm—each the equivalent of three hundred printed pages—contain and preserve millions of entries from family trees whose branches extend throughout much of the civilized world—to the United States, England, Scotland, Wales, Canada, Mexico, France, Germany, Hungary, Denmark, Sweden, Norway, Fiji, Panama, Australia, and New Zealand. In addition, tape-recorded oral genealogies are on file from Tonga, New Zealand, the Cook Islands, the Society Islands, the Austral Islands, and even China, where oral records have been traced back to A.D. 900. Every month, another four thousand microfilm rolls are added to the collection.

The purpose? In Mormon theology, family ties are not generational, but eternal; ideally, all ancestors belong in heaven with their descendants, but this can only be realized if the descendants bond their ancestors to the church in a "sealing" ceremony, a kind of second baptism—and *this* can only be done if the name of the ancestor is known. And so the search goes on, the names pursued with the profound tenacity that has marked the church from its beginning. Superficial logic would suggest that if the search goes on long enough, the name of nearly every human being who has lived on the earth within trackable time ultimately will find its way into the files of Granite Mountain. This seems unlikely.

action that might have been expected of a harassed and persecuted people whose local leaders had been driven to the equivalent of a wartime hysteria by the "invasion" of federal troops. In any case, the massacre did nothing to alleviate tensions between the Mormons and the national government.

In the 1860's and 1870's Congress passed laws to eliminate polygamy and to take the trial of cases of alleged plural marriage out of the hands of the Mormon judges and juries, who invariably failed to convict. With the Edmunds Act of 1882 and the Edmunds-Tucker Act of 1887, Congress began an even more vigorous attack on the Mormon Church and polygamy. Arrest and imprisonment of polygamous Mormon leaders, confiscation of church property, federal control of voting, and invasion by United States marshalls gradually reduced the Mormons' physical ability to resist the imposition upon them of standards of behavior that would be in harmony with the majority of the United States.

Still, polygamy, so long a part of Mormon culture, was difficult to excise; it continued to be practiced, though on a much reduced scale, and the church fought the Edmunds-Tucker Act all the way to the United States Supreme Court. Finally, in 1890, the Court upheld the constitutionality of the act, and the Mormons were beaten. In September of that year, Wilford Woodruff, then president of the church, issued an official declaration: "Inasmuch as laws have been enacted by Congress forbidding plural marriages, which laws have been pronounced constitutional by the court of last resort, I hereby declare my intention to submit to those laws, and to use my influence with the members of the Church over which I preside to have them do likewise." The declaration was unanimously declared "official and binding" by a vote during the October general conference, and the doctrine of plural marriage was no longer officially part of Mormon dogma.

While Woodruff's declaration did not necessarily bring an immediate end to existing polygamous relationships, nevertheless it gave promise that the church would no longer promote the institution, and with polygamy out of the way insofar as politics were concerned, Congress permitted Utah to draft a constitution and become a state in 1896.

What has happened since then is extraordinarily interesting. Having once resolved to surrender on the key issue of polygamy, the Mormon leadership decided further to reduce distrust and dislike by deliberately conforming to the rest of the United States in many other aspects of life. This meant accepting the patterns of thought of Victorian middle-class America, including laissez-faire economics and a hostility to anything that suggested socialism—despite decades of Mormon church socialism. The Mormons' economic cooperatives were allowed to pass into private ownership, to be operated as profit-seeking enterprises, sometimes as the private property of the local or general leaders of the church.

While the private profit motive grew at the expense of the old zeal for communitarian enterprises, Mormons of all levels of income continued to tithe and to devote extraordinary amounts of time to the work of the church. The church continued to be the center of their emotional and social lives. And since the church was so central to the thinking of all practicing Mormons, and since it had always given political leadership in the past, so did it continue to exercise a heavy influence on politics in the new era.

Politically the Mormons had been organized in a party of their own—the so-called Peoples' Party—prior to making peace with the national government. Now the leaders decided that the Mormons would have more influence in Washington if they joined the national parties, dividing more or less equally between the Republicans and Democrats, so that the Mormons would have a solid bloc of votes in both camps. The faithful were solemnly instructed so to do—although in practice the leadership itself tended to find the atmosphere of the Republican party more congenial than that of the Democratic party.

This was only natural, for starting with Nauvoo and the first decade in Utah, there had been a tendency for the men at the head of the Mormon Church to become well-to-do property owners and businessmen. As Horace Greeley, the famous journalist, somewhat acidly remarked after meeting Brigham Young's principal associates in 1859, "their Mormonism has not impoverished them...." By the late nineteenth century this group of prosperous leaders had grown both in wealth and in influence. For them conformity to the mores of Victorian America was no problem once the divisive issue of polygamy was no longer present. In politics their natural allies were the Old Guard Republicans in Washington and in the individual states. In labor relations a comparable affiliation with well-to-do middle-class America also occurred. Since many more of the Mormon leaders of that day belonged to the owner or manager class than to the ranks of the workers, it is understandable why they joined Middle Western and Eastern employers in denouncing labor's attempts to organize.

This tendency to affiliate with the conservative, ruling, entrepreneurial elements of American society was strengthened by at least two factors. One was the relatively provincial setting of most Mormon communities at the turn of the century, even after the arrival of local railroads. The present-day dispersion of Mormons to big cities in non-Mormon regions is a phenomenon that has developed only since the Great Depression and the Second World War. Most Mormons of seventy or eighty years ago still lived in small towns and modest-sized cities that had little communication with the big national and regional centers where, in the age of Theodore Roosevelt and Robert La Follette, liberals and progressives were arguing fiercely over new ideas about social justice and using the power of the state to curb monopoly and economic abuse.

The other factor was a practice established by Brigham Young, who perferred that at his death his successors should be chosen on the basis of seniority. By following this practice, the Mormons have acquired the oldest rulers of any organization known to modern man. To cite recent experience, David O. McKay, who was president of the church for nineteen years, died in 1970 at the age of ninety-six. His successor, Joseph Fielding Smith, was ninety-three when he took over McKay's duties and ninety-five when he died. Smith's successor, Harold B. Lee, was a comparatively youthful seventy-three, yet survived only eighteen months in office. The present head, Spencer W. Kimball, is eighty-two. No matter how great the good will of such men, it is asking too much to

More than a century removed from the days of handcarts, persecution, and poverty, the Mormon Temple outside Washington, D.C., glitters with a modern prosperity.
DAVID HART

expect them to comprehend the attitudes of the great majority of Americans who are young enough to be their children, grandchildren, or even great-grandchildren.

It is almost unnecessary to add that in the general drive to make peace with middle-class America, the old tendency to Mormon separatism has been replaced by an earnest patriotism. Does this mean that the modern Mormons have been fully absorbed into American society? That basic question has deeply concerned a new group of Mormon intellectuals who have become increasingly significant during the past decade. In 1966 this group founded *Dialogue,* a serious journal in which to thrash out the problems they faced in attempting to harmonize the faith, teachings, and practices Joseph Smith had revealed to their forefathers in the 1830's and 1840's, with the harshly insistent conditions of the 1960's and 1970's. The very first issue of this new journal started with an admirable editorial preface that declared:

"Today ... most Mormons live outside Utah.... Today it is not unusual to see Mormon Congressmen in Washington, Mormon business executives in Chicago, Mormon professors at Harvard, or Mormon space scientists at Houston. Mormons are participating freely in the social, economic, and cultural currents of change sweeping twentieth-century America."

Then, with no transition, the editorial suddenly added this assertion:

"But Mormons do remain apart from greater American society. Their experience, heritage, and tradition of years in isolation remain an integral part of Mormon belief; Mormon doctrine reinforces individual withdrawal and defiance of conformity in the face of modern convention. This new era of life in the secular world, far from the cloisters of a Rocky Mountain Zion, has created a host of dilemmas for the individual who seeks to reconcile faith and reason."

All Americans face in some degree the problem of reconciling ancestral faith with contemporary thought and practice. But for the Mormons the problem is more difficult because Mormonism is such a complete way of life. Even though Mormons participate vigorously in the PTA, the Chamber of Commerce, local politics, business, and the professions, they still spend much of their lives in self-contained Mormon groups. From childhood until old age they meet, talk, play, and pray in their own groups. They have their own charities, projects, entertainments. They have elaborate youth programs at high schools and colleges, as part of their campaign to hold their young people in the church (as well as gain new members) during the years when most denominations lose a high percentage of their young men and women.

Where most Americans must find their individual and often lonely ways through this confusing modern era, the Mormons can live in a warmly supportive group atmosphere, if they wish. To break with so all-embracing a pattern is a wrenching, distorting experience. For just that reason independent thinking and modern doubts have come only slowly to most Mormons. It is far easier to conform to the church's omnipresent guidance than to challenge it. At the same time, change is coming to the world with extraordinary speed. The continued subordination of women and blacks, at a time when outside opinion has turned so drastically against discrimination, illustrates the weight of cultural lag within the Mormon community. Will the Mormons be able to work out adjustments to contemporary pressures, without sacrificing the essence of their distinctive and close-knit culture? For the moment, the answer must be in doubt, but in view of the Mormons' record of meeting challenges in the past, it is by no means certain that they will fail.

Rodman W. Paul, who is professor of history at the California Institute of Technology, is the author of several books, including Mining Frontiers of the Far West: 1848–1880 *and* A Victorian Gentlewoman in the Far West: The Reminiscences of Mary Hallock Foote.

For further reading: Great Basin Kingdom, *by Leonard Arrington (Harvard University Press, 1958), and* Mormonism and American Culture, *edited by Marvin S. Hill and James B. Allen (Harper & Row, 1972).*

Our Misplaced President

Roger Darcy Amboy (*b.* 1781?, *d.* 1856?)

by Andrew Ward

Historians are still puzzling over the discovery of an official White House portrait of President Roger Darcy Amboy, who appears to have held our nation's highest office somewhere between Van Buren and Buchanan. Obscured by drapes for over a century, the painting was discovered by an Amboy descendant who had come to urethane the baseboards.

"I am frankly embarrassed," confessed presidential historian T. Fawning Strathalmond. "He was there all along. We just naturally assumed he was Polk."

Little is known as yet about our mystery President. Though there is not a shred of evidence to support it, Roger Darcy Amboy was probably born in the late 1700's in or around Succassuna, New Jersey. The earliest documentation, carbon-dated to about November, 1803, shows an Amboy in Bayonne receiving "seven decapods of barm fortnightly" from the Huckabuck party bigwig, Boss Nib, who would later moneybag Amboy's possible rise to power.

A champion of the bronze standard, Boss Nib broke with the Huckabucks to form his own party, whose members called themselves the Niblickers. There not being sufficient Niblickers to fill a slate, Nib had to dig deep into the ranks of his candlery workers, selecting Amboy (an apprentice dip) to run for the Delaware lieutenant-governorship.

Delaware proved steep going. Amboy couldn't find it until well into the campaign, had no political know-how, and possessed, as one wag put it, "all the stature of a pullet." But Amboy had pluck, and effectively spoke out wherever he went against whatever was handy. One of his speeches, delivered to an assembly of retired parsnippers, was brought to the attention of Daniel Webster, who described it in his diary as "a hodgepodge of mawkish upchuck."

Amboy failed in his Delaware quest, despite his sole opponent's demise in the arms of a common beaverbright hours before the election. Still, he had made something of a name for himself, and Boss Nib recognized his young dip's lambent promise. Outfitting him with teeth, lifts, and a distinctive corn-silk toupee, Nib set Amboy on the road to national prominence. In an era when politicians boasted of their frontier upbringing, Amboy claimed to have been born in a stump and raised by squirrels. Acorns, fern cuttings, and little wooly worms were handed out at his rallies, and Nib blitzed the media with portraits of a bushy Amboy darting from tree to tree as hounds labeled "monarchist," "papist," "tariffist," and "pederast" chased along the ground below.

In the next election, Amboy was nominated Niblick candidate for President, and in that time of rough-and-tumble politics he proved a master. He delighted crowds by speculating as to the ancestry and the cohabitive preferences of his opponent, aging frontier general Mars Dispepys, whom Amboy referred to as "Old Offwhite" and "a variety of fey tumblebug." The general, for his part, threatened to cannonade Amboy's pipkin should he persist in these defamations, but before he could carry out his threat, the old warrior was incapacitated by an attack of the bilge after downing, in one sitting, an entire slump of braised glutcakes. Amboy triumphed by default.

President Roger Darcy Amboy's administration was marked by very little in the way of anything. He immediately set the tone for his Presidency by spending most of his time at the Inaugural keeping an eye on his coat.

Inundated by office seekers from the first day he set foot in the White House, Amboy finally developed a policy of handing out maps. "If they can't find their offices now," he declared to his secretary, "to hell with them."

Boss Nib held sway over Amboy's cabinet. Indeed, the President would sometimes come in to find he had not been allotted a chair, and was often reduced to trying to make himself heard from the window ledge, or while standing around the room, leaning on things. In this relaxed atmosphere, Amboy became a party to several controversial schemes, including a pension fund for the descendants of Hundred Years' War veterans, a Federal Highboy Standardization Authority, and the annexation of the Gulf of Mexico. This latter move was designed to mollify the Slave South, which had been agitated over the annexation of free territories. "For every new acre of free land," proposed Amboy, "let us declare an equal portion of sea-water slave." Historians now believe that had the South accepted Amboy's solution, instead of just standing there, gaping at him, the Civil War might never have happened.

The Amboy White House was the scene of many Washington social functions, some of which involved full-course meals. His First Lady and future wife, Nanky Nib, is said to have been the first to serve dried fruit in the White House, and to have introduced oilcloth, and soap in the shape of animals. Amboy himself was the last of our Presidents to make his own bed.

Still, he never seemed comfortable in his office, perhaps because he had it decorated with rented furniture. As his term drew to a close, Amboy grew less and less accessible, locking himself in his room for whole afternoons to chew on nutmeats and bits of bark. Their pockets stuffed with stationery supplies, his Niblicker cronies soon abandoned government for the richer fields of hoodwinking and carbunklery.

"My friends have deserted me. I feel," a forlorn Amboy confided to his valet in the closing weeks of his Presidency, "like having the open-faced turkey sandwich today, Billy."

Amboy returned briefly to the candlery, but, no longer content with dipping, he retired to the woods near Succassuna where, around 1856, he seems to have disappeared.

Funds for an Amboy monument are being collected by his descendants, and his newly dusted portrait has been moved to its rightful prominence: up there with Polk and Pierce, Taylor and Tyler and Harrison and Fillmore, though not necessarily in that order. "After all," the President declared in his Amboy Day proclamation, "he was our President. Wasn't he?"

Andrew Ward, a free lance in New Haven, Connecticut, is working on Premature Memoirs, *a collection of his humorous pieces.*

The Imprisonment of Lafayette

and how, a decade after the Revolution, a melodramatic rescue attempt, involving a grateful young American, went awry

by James Wesley Baker

Early on the afternoon of June 13, 1777, a French vessel slipped into an isolated inlet on the coast of South Carolina and dropped anchor. On board was the young Marquis de Lafayette, who had purchased the ship for this voyage, along with Baron de Kalb and a group of French nobles, all promised commissions in the "Armies of the States-General of North America" by one of the American agents in Paris, Silas Deane.

The Frenchmen were lost; they had been heading for Charleston, but were driven fifty miles up the coast by contrary winds. As it happened, some slaves belonging to a prominent local patriot, Major Benjamin Huger, were grappling for oysters in the bay. Understanding Lafayette's predicament, they led him and Kalb to their master's plantation, where Kalb was able to explain, in his excellent English, why they had come from France. Major Huger, himself a descendant of French Huguenots, welcomed his unexpected guests and invited them to spend the night at his home.

In time Lafayette, Kalb, and their retinue made their way north, joined the Continental Army, and helped win independence for the United States. But among those who first encountered Lafayette on that night in South Carolina was one of Major Huger's sons, Francis Kinloch Huger, who was then three years old. As a result, seventeen years later young Huger took part in one of the oddest episode's in Lafayette's life—a plot to liberate him from a prison in Austria.

* * * * * *

ILLUSTRATED FOR AMERICAN HERITAGE BY ALAN E. COBER

87

The tale of how, long after the American Revolution, Lafayette came to be incarcerated in the central European country begins during the early events of the French Revolution. The marquis, a leading figure in those events, was a moderate who actively supported the concept of a constitutional monarchy, a position that alienated him from both the royalists and the radicals. He was serving as commanding general of the northern army in France when the "suspension" of the king came, on August 10, 1792. With revolutionaries like Robespierre and Danton in control, Lafayette realized that only the guillotine awaited him in France. He crossed the frontier into the principality of Liège with a group of followers just as the Assembly passed a decree calling for his arrest as a traitor. He hoped to take refuge in a neutral country, but when he reached the Austrian lines he was arrested as an enemy of monarchy and sent to Prussia for temporary confinement.

In London the French aristocrats living in exile were disturbed by the arrest and made efforts through diplomatic channels to have Lafayette freed. Chosen to work as the exiles' agent in Prussia was Justus Erich Bollman, a doctor from Hanover more interested in adventure than in medicine. He had already made a reputation for himself among the exiles by successfully smuggling the ex-minister of war, the Comte de Narbonne, out of France to the refuge of England and the arms of his lover, Madame de Staël.

In early 1794 Bollman was in Berlin appealing for Lafayette's freedom. Unsuccessful there, he then traveled to Prison Magdeburg, where Lafayette had been incarcerated, but he arrived too late. Lafayette was now being held in Neisse and in May was suddenly transferred out of Prussia to an undisclosed Austrian prison. The emperor of Austria held Lafayette personally responsible for the downfall of Louis XVI and was determined not to let the general's friends contact him.

Since Bollman kept no journal during his search for Lafayette, the details of what happened are somewhat hazy. The existing accounts, for the most part, were written years after the events and often differ in details. To ascertain what happened it is necessary to check these later accounts against two important documents that have survived: a message written by Lafayette to Bollman and a transcript of a military examination of young Huger.

Three months after Lafayette's disappearance Bollman's search took him to Olmütz, a fortress city located on a plain in the Moravian section of Austria (now in Czechoslovakia). There the young German heard talk of increased security at the prison because of the recent arrival of some important prisoners—so important, in fact, that they were referred to only by number to conceal their identities. Even the guards were forbidden to talk to the prisoners, who were locked in their cells behind two doors, one of iron, the other of wood. Bollman felt sure Lafayette was among this group.

Bollman checked into the Golden Swan and during his visit made friends with the prison physician, Dr. Haberlein. How they met is not known, although most accounts claim Bollman feigned illness and sent for Haberlein to act as his doctor. What we do know is that Haberlein, a simple, unsuspecting man, was one of the few people aware of the prisoners' identities, and through him Bollman confirmed his suspicion that Lafayette was one of the nameless prisoners of Olmütz.

After their meeting Haberlein became an unwitting accomplice, a messenger transmitting notes and books between Bollman and Lafayette. It all seemed innocent enough. The doctor was permitted and even encouraged to read the letters in order to be assured they were simply friendly notes; but each one contained messages written in one of the simplest forms of disappearing ink, lemon juice.

Austria at the time was full of spies and suspicious officials quick to check on foreigners who stayed too long in sensitive areas such as Olmütz. So Bollman traveled on to Vienna, promising Dr. Haberlein he would return. It was there that he met Francis Kinloch Huger.

Francis' father, Major Huger, had been killed in 1779 during the siege of Charleston, and two years later his wife had shipped young Francis off to England to improve his health. By 1794 he had completed medical studies in London, but before returning to America he decided to see firsthand the war raging in Europe between France and her neighbors. That spring he had set off for Antwerp, the seat of English operations against the French, where he spent several months working in the British hospitals. From there he had moved on to Vienna.

Ready to return to England before sailing for home, the young American was looking for a traveling companion when a mutual friend introduced Bollman to him as a possibility. Speculation on the whereabouts of Lafayette was widespread in Europe, and Huger had more than a passing interest in the topic. He recalled later that it was during his first conversation with Bollman that he mentioned Lafayette's early visit to his home, and wondered out loud about the general's imprisonment. Bollman, not ready to take anyone into his confidence, told Huger only that he would write him in the next eight or ten days with a definite answer about returning with him to England. First, he explained, he had to travel to Hungary.

Huger waited eight days for the letter, then, anxious to get back to London, was ready to purchase a carriage and leave alone, when Bollman showed up at his room.

The German said he would join Huger if he would promise not to repeat what he was about to hear. Huger agreed, and listened as Bollman traced the events of the past few years. He told of finding Lafayette and revealed he had not been in Hungary at all during the past week, but in Olmütz, working out the details of an escape.

Immediately upon returning to the Moravian village, he had contacted Lafayette through Dr. Haberlein, and between them they had worked out a plan.

Every other day, Lafayette was driven into the countryside under close guard, ostensibly for his health. Bollman, he suggested, should overtake the carriage and spirit him away on horseback. The general made it sound easy enough. "We are in a phaeton," he wrote Bollman in the margins of a book; "nobody with me but the corporal—who, by the by, is afflicted with a rupture—and a clumsy driver. . . . Have a trusty man with you. Stop the driver. I engage to . . . frighten the little cowardly corporal with his own sword. . . ." He suggested they bring a third horse, saying: "I will not have the least difficulty to jump on a led horse of your man. . . ."

Lafayette left it to Bollman to work out the details and plan the escape route. No mention was made of a specific meeting place or of a contingency plan should anything go wrong. It was arranged, however, that when all was ready Bollman would wait beside the road and, when Lafayette's carriage passed, make a signal with his handkerchief. This would indicate the attempt was to be made two days later.

When Bollman had explained the plan to Huger, he put the question: Would Huger join the enterprise? It was almost a matter of family pride for Huger. As he said later, "I saw an opportunity to restore liberty to a man who at my own age had risked everything for me."

Nineteenth-century accounts of the events of the next few days read like a spy novelette, complete with a custom-made coach containing secret compartments for ropes and saws. But in truth, very little of what happened in the days before the escape is known. It is certain, however, that Bollman and Huger checked in at the Golden Swan in Olmütz on November 5, 1794. The next day they sat on their horses by the side of the road waiting for Lafayette to take his drive in the country. When the carriage passed, the prearranged handkerchief signal was given, letting the general know that the escape would come two days later.

On Saturday morning, November 8, Huger and Bollman paid their bill and sent a servant ahead to Hoff, a village twenty-five miles down the road on the way to the border. Then they set out to watch for Lafayette's carriage. Afraid of arousing suspicion, they had decided against taking a third horse as Lafayette had suggested; instead Huger rode a horse that was trained to carry two riders. Lafayette would ride alone on Bollman's horse while his rescuers followed on the other.

After going a few miles down the road without seeing the carriage, the conspirators decided they must have missed it and headed back to town. On the way they met the coach. The corporal sat beside Lafayette. The driver sat in front, and another soldier rode behind the carriage. Bollman and Huger continued down the road a short distance, then turned and trotted after the carriage. When it halted by the roadside, they also stopped and watched as Lafayette and the corporal got out, began walking through a field, and then paused, engaged in conversation.

At that point Huger and Bollman spurred their horses, galloping up as Lafayette pulled the corporal's sword out of its sheath. But the "little cowardly corporal" failed to be frightened; instead, he grabbed the sword blade, cutting his hands, and yelled for help. Peasants working in nearby fields looked up, but merely watched the struggle; the driver also failed to answer the call. Only the other soldier took action, heading back toward the fortress, shouting and waving his hat to attract the attention of the sentries on the walls of the fortress, which was some distance off but still visible across the flat plain.

Lafayette's miscalculation of the character of the corporal led to a rapid series of unexpected complications in the plan. Instead of being able to hold him at bay with the sword, the general was struggling with the corporal for its possession. Bollman rode up to help Lafayette, leaped from his horse, and threw the reins to Huger. Frightened by the clamor, the horse lurched—and Huger watched helplessly as it galloped away. Bollman pulled the corporal away from Lafayette, but the tough little man gave up the sword only to seize Lafayette by the cravat. The general weakly cried, *"Il m'étrangle!"*—"He's strangling me!"—as Huger joined the fight, first being careful to pass his arm through his mount's bridle. Failing to intimidate the corporal with a pistol, Huger stuffed it back into his pocket and managed to pull the bloody hands away from the general's throat. Lafayette, evidently in poor shape from the encounter, fell to the ground as Bollman dragged the corporal down, pinning him and pushing a handkerchief into his mouth.

Huger helped Bollman keep the guard subdued as Lafayette struggled back to his feet. Huger then shouted to

Lafayette to take his horse and "get to Hoff," the village where the servant had been sent. The general mounted and started to trot away, then stopped, apparently unwilling to leave the two behind. Waving him on, Huger anxiously repeated "get to Hoff!" and the marquis rode off. Bollman and Huger conferred for a moment and then released the corporal, who took off on foot after his escaped charge.

A peasant boy had managed to stop Bollman's frightened horse and was returning with the prize when Huger spotted him. Calling to his companion, the American ran to the horse and had mounted it by the time Bollman was helped up behind him by the obliging boy. With Lafayette still visible on the road ahead, they urged their horse forward to catch up with him.

Unfortunately Bollman's horse, unlike Lafayette's, was unused to the double load. When urged faster than a trot, he gave a buck that dumped Bollman, who was then unable to climb back up. Huger dismounted and helped his companion into the saddle. Their progress had been so slow that when Huger mounted behind Bollman, he was helped by the same peasant boy, who had been following them on foot. Bollman pushed the horse into a gallop and it again bucked, throwing both of them. This time Huger told Bollman to take the horse and follow Lafayette. He would follow on foot.

After Bollman had ridden off, Huger ran along a road leading to the mountains. Just when he thought he was safe, he heard shouting and looked back to see three men running after him. He began to run again, hoping to reach the mountains and slip into Prussian Silesia, but he was overtaken by a peasant on horseback who had joined the chase. Seeing that it was impossible to escape, Huger gave himself up to the horseman. The three on foot joined them, and Huger was escorted back to Olmütz, where he was turned over to soldiers.

He was immediately taken before General D'Arco, the commandant of the fortress, for examination. D'Arco's reputation was certain to be tarnished by the escape of such an important prisoner, and he was determined to uncover the whole plot. Huger answered the often pointed questions truthfully and in some detail, telling of his meeting with Bollman and the events surrounding the escape itself. He said he felt justified in what he had done: "I did not think of harming any one; and I was assured that it was the purpose of M. Lafayette to cross immediately to America and not to mix himself any more in the affairs of the Empire."

This ingenuous argument did nothing to help Huger's case. D'Arco noted at the end of the transcript of the examination: "The culprit was turned over by the military authorities to the ordinary Olmütz court, put in irons, as a criminal, and held in the strictest custody." All Huger's possessions were taken, an iron was put around an ankle, another around a wrist, and he was chained to a staple in the wall over the wooden bench that served as his bed.

Lafayette, meanwhile, was alone in an unfamiliar area. The only times he had been allowed outside his cell had been for the carriage rides, which never took him more than three miles from the fortress, and Hoff was twenty-five miles away. Complicating matters further, Bollman had never told Lafayette what escape route they would follow. Indeed, it appears that during the confusion resulting from the corporal's resistance, Lafayette had misunderstood Huger's frantic advice for him to "get to Hoff." Not recognizing the name of the city, he thought the American had simply told him to "get off." Separated from his guides, the general reached a fork and chose the road leading him away from Hoff and the waiting coach.

Covered with mud and blood from the fight, he rode into a village and offered two thousand crowns for a fresh horse. The large sum, his accent, and his disheveled appearance aroused suspicion, and he was taken into custody. Brought before the mayor for an examination, he kept a cool head, gave a plausible explanation, and was about to be released when someone in the crowd recognized him. The general first denied the identification, but when the mayor insisted he be taken to Olmütz to make certain, he admitted that he was indeed Lafayette, and was escorted back to his cell.

Bollman was the only one to reach Hoff. Not finding Lafayette there, he guessed that the general had gotten lost. Crossing the border into Silesia, he searched for Lafayette, hoping he had been able to make it into Prussia along a different route. A week later, Bollman, too, was arrested, and after two weeks he was taken to Olmütz to join Huger.

In the meantime the civil examination of Huger had begun. Since Huger spoke no German, a Professor Passi, a tutor employed by a Russian nobleman living in the vicinity of Olmütz, served as interpreter.

For three months Huger and Bollman were kept in solitude and brought separately before the tribunal for examination. The early investigation centered on a suspected political plot involving Austrians. Finally the judges determined the two had worked independently of any local help and for the sole purpose of freeing Lafayette. The charges were reduced to "forcing a military post," and after that they were allowed a little more freedom and better food. But the examinations continued, this time on the revised charge.

There were efforts on many fronts to help the two. Huger managed to smuggle letters out to Thomas Pinckney, former governor of South Carolina, who was then the American minister in London. He first wrote him on January 5, 1795, asking Pinckney to write his mother and closing with the plea "Don't forget us."

At home Huger's family wrote to George Washington, asking that the President intervene to obtain his freedom. Secretary of State Timothy Pickering informed them that the President was concerned, but "the cause of Mr. Huger's confinement would render an application delicate and difficult, the United States having no public functionary in the Austrian dominions. . . ."

In Olmütz the prisoners had more influential help. Their interpreter had hinted several times that there were friends working in their behalf. It seems that Passi's regular employer, a certain Count Mitrowsky, took a sympathetic interest in the case. He gave Passi the money necessary to bribe the judges, and when Bollman and Huger were found guilty the sentence was unusually light: one month's labor in irons, followed by banishment from Austria. With a little more encouragement from Mitrowsky the judges saw fit to reduce the sentence to fourteen days' further confinement and banishment. Eight months after the attempted rescue Huger and Bollman were released.

Passi made all necessary arrangements for them, allowing them to see their benefactor briefly, then hurrying them across the border. They left none too soon. The crown lawyers had reported to Vienna, and a directive came back upbraiding the judges for their leniency and demanding that the trial be reopened.

Lafayette continued to be held prisoner until a young French general named Bonaparte invaded the Austrian dominions in 1797, forcing the emperor to sue for peace. The Directory told Bonaparte to demand the release of Lafayette and the others at Olmütz as a condition to a peace settlement. The famous general was freed September 19, 1797, five years after his arrest along the frontier.

But the story does not quite end there. Following their release from prison Bollman sailed with Huger to the United States in 1796. Afer failing repeatedly in business ventures, he became an agent of Aaron Burr in 1805. He first served the former Vice President as a land promoter but soon became entangled in Burr's alleged scheme to establish a western empire in the Louisiana Territory. In late 1806, shortly after delivering an incriminating message from Burr to General James Wilkinson, Bollman was arrested and—for the second time in twelve years—imprisoned. He declined Jefferson's offer of a pardon on the ground that it would be tantamount to an admission of guilt, but regained his freedom when the case against Burr failed to stand up. In his later years he wrote several pamphlets on the banking systems of the United States and England; he died in Jamaica in 1821.

Huger, meanwhile, had finished work on his degree in 1797, graduating from the medical school of the University of Pennsylvania. He returned to South Carolina, married one of Thomas Pinckney's daughters, and divided his time between his plantation on the Santee River and a summer home in Statesburg, choosing the life of a rice farmer instead of that of a doctor; he also served two terms in the South Carolina legislature.

Then in 1824 Lafayette arrived in America for a tour that took him to every part of the country. After landing in New York City he got in touch with Huger, with whom he had previously corresponded. Referring to him as "my dear deliverer," Lafayette asked him to join his party in New York. Huger did so and then accompanied the general to Yorktown for special ceremonies there.

In 1825 Huger again joined Lafayette during his visit to South Carolina. Meeting in Columbia, they traveled to Charleston, where Huger's friends and neighbors in the port city considered him a tie between their city and "the guest of the nation" and made a point of including him in the celebration. Auguste Levasseur, a member of Lafayette's official party, wrote: "At the dinner, at the theatre, and the ball, in short every where, the name of Huger was inscribed with that of Lafayette. . . ."

The story of an American who was sent to prison because he attempted to rescue Lafayette had a romantic appeal and was mentioned in many of the popular though not always accurate accounts of the general's life that appeared in the mid-1820's. There was even a popular play, entitled *Lafayette, or the Castle of Olmütz*. The rather free adaptation of the events amused Huger. An admirer in Boston asked if he was the hero. He replied: "Oh, no, indeed. Heroes are always married at the end of the play and I am not so fortunate. I am represented, however, as desperately in love with the daughter of the governor of the castle, and I am left in the same unhappy situation at the end of the play."

Huger remained a retiring, modest man until his death in 1855. Although he was willing to tell the story of his youthful adventure to those who asked, he said of himself: "I simply considered myself the representative of the young men of America, and acted accordingly."

James Wesley Baker, a free-lance writer from Eastover, S.C., specializes in the colonial and Revolutionary history of the South.

Arthur S. Mole

Mole's Other Masterpieces

The question of how many angels can dance on the point of a pin stimulated debate among medieval scholars. Absurd, we say. But before we chortle, we might recall that a latter-day photographer once spent his time figuring how many men would be required to form a giant profile of Uncle Sam or a really big Liberty Bell.

The camera artist's name was Arthur S. Mole, and in our December issue we published his living portrait of Woodrow Wilson (right). Interested readers from all over the country wrote in about it, prompting us to publish a further sampling of Mole's monumental images.

Mole—who is eighty-eight and now lives in Florida—made about forty such photographs at military camps during World War I, shooting from specially constructed towers that were 65 to 85 feet high.

Perspective posed a special problem for him. The design had to be staked out on the ground according to an outline drawn on the glass of Mole's 11 by 14 inch view camera. In the case of the Liberty Bell, for example, one eyewitness—M. M. Cosgrove of Ossining, New York—points out that the length of the beam across the top was 368 feet, but the width of the bell at the bottom was only 64 feet.

Another reader, Bob Lee, editor of Black Hills Publishers, Inc., of Sturgis, South Dakota, interviewed Fred Young, a ninety-year-old veteran who had appeared in one of Mole's photographs. "Mr. Young," Lee writes, "said the formation was reflective of the discipline so prevalent in the Army at that time. He regrets that this sort of discipline appears to have diminished among young people of today."

Eyes right: Reclining doughboys compose Uncle Sam's beard, shot at Camp Lee, Virginia; the flag, Mole's first creation, was photographed at the Great Lakes Naval Training Center; Camp Dodge, Iowa, set the scene for Miss Liberty; the Liberty Bell, Mole's largest work (twenty-five thousand men), was photographed at Camp Dix, New Jersey.

READERS' ALBUM

BIG BIRD

We don't suppose there has ever been such a thing as a "Best Chicken Photograph" contest—although in a country as dedicatedly contest-minded as these United States it would not come as much of a surprise. In any case, there is little doubt in our minds that the picture above would win such a competition with little or no difficulty. Ulrich Bourgeois was the photographer, obviously a master of his craft, a man to make all other chicken photographers cringe with envy. The picture was taken in Manchester, New Hampshire, in 1901, and was but one of many that Bourgeois produced for the postcard division of the John D. Varick Company of Boston. The pudgy rascal in the wagon, apparently getting ready to goad the rooster into mobility, is little John Cartier, a member of one of the many French-Canadian familes that had settled in Manchester. About the rooster himself we know next to nothing—except that he was a really big bird, obviously a pet, and the pride, so we are told, of the Cartier family. Well, why not? Perhaps they couldn't afford a goat.

* * * * *

This picture was sent to us by Martin Sandler of Newtonville, Massachusetts, and we continue to invite our readers to submit unusual, dramatic, or "what's going on here?" photographs that they might own. Such photographs should be at least thirty years old, sharp and clear, and have some interesting story connected with them. They should be sent to Geoffrey C. Ward, American Heritage Publishing Co., 10 Rockefeller Plaza, N.Y., N.Y. 10020.

As we cannot be responsible for original material, we request that a copy be sent first. Under no circumstances should glass negatives be mailed. Pictures can be returned only if accompanied by a stamped, self-addressed envelope. AMERICAN HERITAGE will pay $50.00 for each one used.

CROSSWORDS IN HISTORY

AMERICAN SPORTS

by Eugene T. Maleska

ACROSS

1. Gabe——, general manager of the N.Y. Yankees
5. Bell captain's call
10. Bowl at Jacksonville
15. Billiards shot
19. Shot and shell
20. Angler for congers
21. Honor as divine
22. Soccer superstar
23. Former N.Y. Giant, now in pro football's Hall of Fame
25. N.I.T. champs in 1956
27. Irish seaport
28. Skater Hamill's new status
30. Pool-parlor game
31. Emulated Willie Shoemaker
32. Regatta entry
34. Feeling nothing
35. One of the "400"
38. Abominator
41. Steal game
44. "Queer duck"
46. Tennis do-overs
47. Opposite of neg.
49. Tod——, famed jockey
51. "M*A*S*H" actor
52. Musical key
54. At the peak
55. Theater section
56. Took in a game
57. Springtime in Paris
58. Ku Kluxers' beliefs
61. Football announcer Summerall
62. "Whiz Kids" of 1950
64. Purdue's team
66. De Gaulle's birthplace
67. Malayan state
68. Tool for boring
69. He said: "Hit 'em where they ain't."
72. Isaac's Esau (as compared with Jacob)
75. Witch bird
76. Where Asmara is
77. Society's riffraff
78. SMU rival
79. College team called The Sioux: Abbr.
81. Fisherman's bait
82. Vast number
83. Polo team
84. Track official
86. "Fistivity" finales
87. Javanese carriage
88. Angry looks
90. He plays Mary's boss on TV
92. Former A.L. team
95. Golfer with an "army"
96. Talent, in China
98. Slews; oodles
99. Feudal serf
101. Important activity for building future teams
105. Poetry: Abbr.
106. College team from Buffalo
110. World Series champs: 1975–76
112. The Bengals of the Big Sky Conference
114. Giant of Biblical days
115. Strange
116. Guard an opponent
117. "Cielo——," aria from *La Gioconda*
118. Gainsay
119. Tackles
120. City in New Hampshire
121. Bowl calls

DOWN

1. Cowboy's buddy
2. Señor's love
3. Ornamental knob on a shield
4. "The Toe" of field-goal fame
5. Honored with entertainment
6. Covered with thatch
7. Stewpot
8. In the: It.
9. Mel——, former N.Y. Giant fullback
10. Lummox
11. Ruckus; fuss
12. P.G.A. player's circuit
13. Famous hunter
14. Take ten
15. Preacher Roe threw one
16. Hindu caste
17. Isomeric
18. "It might have——"
24. A.L. pitching champ in 1915
26. We go: Sp.
29. Welterweight champ: 1934–38
32. Emulate base runner Brock
33. Speech delivered by coach George Allen
35. Breathless, as a miler
36. Biblical pause
37. Baseball's "Splendid Splinter"
39. World Series pitcher: 1976
40. ——Arledge, inventor of instant replay
42. Site of baseball's Hall of Fame
43. Ishmael's mother
45. Fan hurling invectives
48. Spun like Namath's passes
50. N.B.A. team
53. This follows a safety, in football
54. "——needs a good memory": Quintilian
57. "Firechief" Reynolds, of pitching fame
58. "Land of the Morning Calm"
59. Blurry streaks
60. Sorcerers of a sort
63. "Diamond" gal
64. Brazilian port
65. Prefix with "plunk"
67. One in the library
69. Desire
70. Where to hunt tigers
71. Character of a people
72. Tennis boo-boo
73. Caesar's eyes
74. Cavell was one
77. Fuddy-duddies
80. The Wildcats from Lexington
82. Three goals by one player, in ice hockey
83. Ranger of a kind
85. ——del cibo (trattoria leftovers)
87. Umpire's palms-down signal
89. Word with Major or Minor
91. Caused a muddy field
93. Forces afloat
94. Skua or jaeger
97. Kind of tube
100. Siesta sound
101. Warm-water fish
102. Madrid movie house
103. ——even keel
104. Ypremian of the Dolphins
106. Bats' home
107. Van Druten's "——Camera"
108. The Utes play here
109. Indian weights
111. Weak or short foul ball
113. Hunter's quarry

Of herbal medicine,
a "doctor" named Samuel Thomson,
and a sure cure for almost everything...

Belly-My-Grizzle

by Spencer Klaw

Lobelia, the emetic herb favored by Samuel Thomson in his medical treatment, appears above and, aptly, in his right hand in the portrait. It was known as Indian tobacco, Eyebright, and ... belly-my-grizzle.

In the late 1820's and 1830's American physicians found themselves with a major rebellion on their hands. The rebels were their own patients, or ex-patients, and the rebel leader was a onetime New Hampshire farmer and itinerant herb-and-root doctor named Samuel Thomson, who had published, in 1822, a book called *Thomson's New Guide to Health; or, Botanic Family Physician.*

On Thomson's recommendation, hundreds of thousands of Americans were no longer calling in conventionally trained and licensed physicians when they were sick. Instead, they were either doctoring themselves according to the instructions contained in the *New Guide to Health,* or were consulting disciples of Thomson who had set themselves up in business as botanic healers.

It was Thomson's passionate conviction that most physicians of the day were no better than torturers and murderers. Their chief crime against suffering humanity, he argued, was their insistence on dosing patients with "metallic" medicines, by which he mainly meant calomel, a widely used and horribly effective cathartic whose active ingredient was mercury. In Thomson's view, the way to cope with illness was to administer certain herbal remedies—he particularly favored lobelia, a powerful emetic—and to put the patient in a steam bath to make him sweat. Thomson held that it was possible by using these methods to cure every disease known to man, from dyspepsia and croup to cancer and tuberculosis.

Thomson's rebellion was launched at a time when American physicians had been trying, with some success, to enhance their status (and incomes) by putting the practice of medicine on a more professional footing. Before the Revolution, and for some time afterward, in most parts of America anyone with a mind to do so had been at liberty to treat sick people and to call himself a doctor. But in the early 1800's the country's "regular" physicians, led by graduates of the medical schools of Columbia, Harvard, and the University of Pennsylvania, set out to change this. At their behest, state after state established licensing requirements for physicians and imposed penalties on persons practicing medicine without a license. At the same time, new medical schools were founded in the South and West, and young men were entering the profession in such numbers as to assure, before many more years, an adequate supply of licensed physicians for all but the most remote and sparsely settled regions of the country.

The nation's growing medical establishment began to react vigorously—and understandably—to the threat that Thomson posed to its members' self-esteem and to their pocketbooks. His notions about medicine were denounced as at once laughable and dangerous. In a book called *Humbugs of New-York* a New York physician named David Meredith Reese expressed the prevailing view in medical circles when he dismissed Thomsonian practitioners as uneducated quacks, noting by way of proof that their principal remedies were commonly known "by the classical and euphonious names of *screw augur! ram-cat!* and *hell-scraper!*" These names clearly point to the emetic action of lobelia, which was also known, for reasons that are not so clear, as "belly-my-grizzle."

Reese went on to charge that if anyone was killing innocent patients, it was the Thomsonians, whose medicine, he explained, had "systematic arrangements for clandestinely murdering its victims" in infirmaries where patients were "taken care of on the Thomsonian plan, until they either run away... or are quietly buried." (Thomson himself, early in his career, had been tried for the murder of one of his patients.) State and local medical societies called on the authorities to deal harshly with unlicensed practitioners, and some Thomsonians were actually thrown into jail.

But such tactics were unavailing. Between 1822 and 1839 the *New Guide to Health* went through thirteen editions and sold more than 100,000 copies. This was an astonishing total considering that the population of the United States in 1839 was less than seventeen million, and that a copy cost twenty dollars.

Thomsonians also founded, and supported with their subscriptions, some forty journals in which the theory and practice of Thomsonian medicine were expounded. Their pages were filled with stories of the miraculous healing powers of Thomsonian remedies. Typically these accounts told of patients who had been left for dead by their regular doctors—the latter were customarily referred to in terms like "these slick-tongued, high-minded, small-pill-bag, metallic gentry"—and had been restored to robust health within twenty-four hours after swallowing their first dose of belly-my-grizzle. In one variation of the formula it was reported that an old lady in Crawford County, Missouri, had polished off most of a bottle of tincture of lobelia under the mistaken impression that it was whiskey. "I thought I would die," she was said to have told a local Thomsonian practitioner. "But sir, I did not die; for I commenced puking... and please God, sir, I have not had one hour's sickness since."

By the 1830's Thomson was claiming three million followers. This was doubtless an exaggeration, but there were parts of the country where a very large percentage of the populace was taking steam baths and lobelia. They included Mississippi, whose governor gave it as his opinion in 1835 that half the people of his state were Thomsonians. In that same year, regular physicians in Ohio were said to have conceded that one out of three Ohioans had deserted to the enemy. And while steam doctors, as Thomsonian practitioners were often called, were most numerous in the South and West, they did a thriving business in some Eastern cities such as Boston, where it was estimated that by the late 1820's ten thousand of the town's sixty thousand inhabitants had been won over by Thomson.

As the metallic gentry took pleasure in pointing out, Thomson's ideas appealed most strongly to the poor and uneducated. But there were many exceptions. The noted Cincinnati physician Daniel Drake observed sadly in 1829 that the vogue for Thomsonian medicine "was not at present limited to the vulgar. Respectable and intelligent mechaniks, legislative and judicial officers, both state and federal, barristers, ladies, ministers of the gospel, and even some of the medical profession... have become its converts and puffers."

Thomson's ideas fitted in beautifully with the spirit of Jacksonian democracy. Self-educated and self-made, Thomson argued that a free people could well dispense not just with doctors, but with lawyers and ministers and all other specially educated and, in his view, parasitic professional castes. It was all right with him if someone who had carefully studied his *New Guide to Health* should choose to apply its teachings to the cure of disease in others. But he thought it was much better for people to learn how to cure themselves, and toward the end of his life he was deeply troubled because some of his followers, including his own son John, wanted to establish Thomsonian medical schools. Such schools, he feared, would spawn a new elite, and "the benefit of my discoveries will be taken from the people generally, and, like all other crafts, monopolized by a few learned individuals."

But the egalitarian mood of the United States in the late 1820's and 1830's does not alone explain the remarkable popularity of Thomson's ideas. Quite apart from the way people had come to feel about bankers and lawyers, Americans had a specific—and justified—grudge against the medical profession. For this was the golden age of heroic medicine, when doctors were taught that it was their duty, at the first signs of illness, to attack it with harsh therapies—therapies that seldom did any good, and that were often far more unpleasant, and sometimes far more dangerous, than the illness itself.

One of the doctor's most trusted weapons in combating disease was the lancet, which was commonly used in treating even the most trivial disorders. "I remember that a horse kicked me once as Dr. Colby was passing the house," a survivor of the age of blood-letting wrote years later. "I was not injured much, yet mother called in the doctor, and he at once proceeded to bleed me—I presume on general principles."

Bleeding did tend to reduce a fever. But it often did so at the price of a throbbing headache and an overwhelming feeling of weakness, and it seems to have had no other beneficial effects. Bleeding was also dangerous. Many doctors believed in letting the blood flow until the patient lost consciousness, and some patients lost their lives as well. Reminiscing in 1878 about medical practice in Ohio in the first quarter of the nineteenth century, a contributor to the *Cincinnati Lancet and Clinic* recalled "a neighboring physician who proposed to cure and did cure common intermittent [*i.e.*, malaria] by blood-letting alone; he bled the patient till he was too weak to shake, and then the disease and the patient went off together." Physicians in Thomson's time also tormented patients by raising huge blisters on their bodies, breaking the blisters, and then irritating the resulting sores, a procedure that sometimes led to the development of ulcers and gangrene.

More widespread than either bleeding or blistering, and probably more dangerous as well, was the practice of stuffing sick people with calomel. Unpleasant even when taken in small quantities, in the huge doses favored by many doctors it often had terrible side effects on the patient's mouth and salivary glands. "It is but the other day," a Dr. G. C. Howard wrote in the *Boston Medical and Surgical Journal* in 1835, "that I saw a case of gastroenteritis, in which calomel was pushed till the countenance exhibited a most frightful appearance, owing to the excessive swelling of the cheeks, lips, tongue . . . and throat, while the saliva flowed in streams." Many doctors regarded these classic symptoms of mercury poisoning as hopeful signs that the drug was doing its work.

Howard, one of the few regular physicians who did not share the prevailing enthusiasm for calomel, went on to point out that patients who asked why they had to take the stuff did so at their peril. Their doctors, he wrote, "in the plenitude of their wisdom and power, are determined to inflict summary vengeance on them for their temerity and doubt, by a ten times more frequent and greater use of the article in question, than they otherwise would have done."

While most physicians were satisfied that bleeding, blistering, and purging were good for their patients, they did not agree on just why this should be so. Some believed, with the celebrated Dr. Benjamin Rush of Philadelphia, that virtually all disease was caused by an overstimulation of the blood vessels, and that this, in turn, was the result of too much blood in the system, a condition that the physician was in a position to correct with his lancet. (In cases of serious illness Rush advised tapping as much as four-fifths of the patient's blood supply—not all at once, to be sure, but in fairly short order.)

Other doctors had other theories, equally bizarre. Only a few were inclined to agree with Thomas Jefferson, who scoffed at all contemporary theory-spinners and put forward the radical notion that in many cases the physician's proper office was to stand aside and let nature do the healing.

Thomson, too, was a theory-spinner. Like Rush, he held that all disease stemmed from a single cause. In Thomson's view, that cause was a lack of bodily heat, brought about by the body's failure to digest food properly. Consequently the first step in a course of Thomsonian therapy was usually to steam the patient thoroughly.

"When the sweat rolls off as thick as your finger," a Maryland man noted in 1837, in a letter to his son, "the body is washed with cold water and the patient is straightway put to bed with hot bricks to bring back his heat. Then a powerful vomitive is administered, composed of *bay berry,* of cayenne (red pepper) and lobelia, which suffer naught impure to remain in the stomach, and all these herbs are mixed in 40 proof brandy, after which warm water is drunk until there has ensued the most extraordinary vomiting. Next, the patient rises and takes a second bath, like the first. He takes again to his bed, after having been laved with cold water and is surrounded with hot bricks and remains in bed for an hour. At the end of this time he takes two injections [*i.e.*, enemas] of penny royal, cayenne pepper and lobelia and the treatment is over for the day." Thomson also recommended various mild tonics, such as tincture of myrrh, "to give tone to the stomach and bowels, and prevent mortification."

All this was no more likely to cure a patient than bleeding or purging him. But Thomson's system had several advantages over conventional therapies. One was that a family owning a copy of the *New Guide to Health,* which even gave detailed instructions for building a home steam bath, did not need to call in a doctor when someone was sick. Another advantage was that Thomsonian remedies were relatively easy on the patient. There were practitioners, it is true, who tended to pour on the lobelia. Thomson sternly chided one such enthusiast who gave a patient nineteen treatments of Thomsonian medicine in a six-week period "and then left her in a very weak and low condition (no wonder)." But in the dosages recommended by Thomson, lobelia was not nearly as hard on the system as calomel.

Thomson's do-it-yourself treatise was not the first book of its kind to come on the market. But it differed from earlier guides to botanic healing in that it included a lengthy autobiographical sketch, titled "Narrative of the Life and Medical Discoveries of the Author." And the book's popularity no doubt stemmed in part from the pleasure many Americans got from Thomson's account of how a poor and uneducated farm boy, forced to rely on his native wit and powers of observation, nevertheless grew up to expose the greed and wrongheadedness of the medical profession.

Thomson was born in Alstead, New Hampshire, in February, 1769. As he tells it in the "Narrative," he attached himself in very early childhood to a local herb doctor, an old woman named Benton. When she went out to collect roots and herbs, Thomson writes, "she would take me with her, and learn me their names, with what they were good for; and I used to be

Nymphaea odorata
White pond lily

Rubus strigosus
Red raspberry

Solanum dulcamara
Bittersweet, Woody nightshade

Capsicum annuum
Cayenne or Guinea red pepper

The Thomsonian Materia Medica of 1841 included a great variety of flora—among them the eight on these pages—that Thomson recommended for a remarkable range of ailments. White pond lily could be used in a "syrup" to "clear the coats of the stomach and bowels of canker." Red raspberry, Thomson said, was "the best thing for a woman in travail of any article I know of." Lady slipper helped "to quiet mental and nervous irritability." Marsh rosemary was "much esteemed as a gargle." Bittersweet in an ointment would remove "stiffness of the joints, callouses, strains, and relax contracted muscles." Cayenne pepper promoted "free perspiration" by producing a "severe sense of heat in the mouth and stomach, and a genial glow over the whole system." Thomson prescribed slick sumac "to scour the alimentary canal of its viscid coating," and a tea brewed from witch hazel for "bleeding at the stomach and lungs."

Cypripedium pubescens
Lady slipper, Nerve root

Statice limonium
Marsh rosemary, Sea lavender

Rhus glabra
Slick or Small sumac

Hamamelis virginica
Witch hazel

very curious in my inquiries, and in tasting every thing that I found."

One plant that he soon tasted was lobelia. He was four years old at the time, he recalls, and had gone to look for his father's cows. While on this errand "I discovered a plant which had a singular branch and pods... and I had the curiosity to pick some of the pods and chew them; the taste and operation produced, was so remarkable, that I never forgot it." Later, Thomson adds, he "used to induce other boys to chew it, merely by way of sport, to see them vomit."

But it was not until some twenty years had passed that Thomson was persuaded that lobelia, a smallish plant with pale blue blossoms, could do more than just make people sick to their stomachs. There was, and is, disagreement as to whether Thomson was the first to use lobelia as a medicine. Lobelia is also called Indian tobacco, and it was well known to the Penobscot Indians before Thomson was born, although it is not clear whether they took it as a medicine or dried its leaves and smoked them.

However that may be, Thomson's discovery of its curative powers was made on a summer day while he was cutting hay. As he recalls the incident in the "Narrative," he cut a sprig of lobelia and offered it to one of his fellow mowers with the suggestion that he eat it. "When we had got to the end of the piece, which was about six rods," Thomson writes, "he said that he believed what I had given him would kill him, for he never felt so in his life. I looked at him and saw that he was in a most profuse perspiration... he trembled very much, and there was no more color in him than a corpse. I told him to go to the spring and drink some water; he attempted to go, and got as far as the wall, but was unable to get over it, and laid down on the ground and vomited several times."

Fortunately this medical experiment ended happily. Thomson helped his companion into the house, "and in about two hours he ate a very hearty dinner, and in the afternoon was able to do a good half day's labor. He afterwards told me that he never had any thing do him so much good in his life; his appetite was remarkably good, and he felt better than he had for a long time."

Soon afterward Thomson discovered the virtues of steam when he was able to cure his two-year-old daughter of a disease he diagnosed as canker-rash by steaming her every two hours for a week. As word of his prowess as a healer got around, more and more people began coming to him for help, and in 1805 he gave up farming altogether and became a full-time herb doctor, treating patients in Vermont, Massachusetts, and Maine, as well as in New Hampshire. Wherever he went he ran into fierce opposition from regular physicians, one of whom, according to Thomson, tried to kill him with a scythe as he was passing by the physician's door in Eastport, Maine. In Salisbury, Massachusetts, on the complaint of a Dr. French, Thomson was arrested for the murder of a young man named Ezra Lovett, whom he was alleged to have killed with an overdose of lobelia. For more than a month in the cold fall of 1809 he was confined to a filthy and verminous cell in the Newburyport, Massachusetts, jail, where he had no chair, no table, no fire, no candle, no bed, and only a thin and dirty blanket.

Thomson was eventually acquitted after a character witness took from the hand of the prosecutor a sample of the drug with which Thomson was said to have done the deed and ate it in open court. When Thomson had recovered from the effects of his confinement he resumed his work as a peripatetic healer, and the closing pages of the "Narrative" are richly freighted with stories of his therapeutic triumphs. To give just one example, Thomson tells of a young man who was being treated by Thomson's enemy, Dr. French, following an accident in which three of his fingers had been cut to the bone. After three weeks, upon being advised by Dr. French that he should have the fingers amputated, the patient consulted Thomson; ten days later, with all fingers intact, he was back on his job in a nail factory. Soon afterward, when Thomson asked how his fingers were, "he said they were perfectly cured; he wished to know what my bill was for attending him. I asked him what Dr. French had charged, and he said he had sent his bill to his mother, amounting to seventeen dollars; I told him I thought that was enough for us both, and that I should charge him nothing. His mother was a poor widow depending on her labor and that of her son for a living."

Thomson's robust egalitarianism was coupled with a shrewd business sense. In 1813, nine years before the publication of his *New Guide to Health*, he had hit on an ingenious scheme for propagating, and profiting from, his ideas. He patented his therapeutic discoveries, and began selling certificates that conferred on the purchaser "the right of preparing and using, for himself and family, the medicine and System of Practice secured to Samuel Thomson by Letters Patent from the President of the United States...."

A certificate, or "right," cost twenty dollars, and with it the purchaser got written instructions in the principles of Thomsonian medicine. At first these instructions were contained in *The Medical Circular*, a pamphlet that Thomson had drafted while lying on the floor of his Newburyport jail cell. Later, however, each purchaser of a right got a copy of the *New Guide to Health*. To push the sale of his rights, Thomson appointed regional agents—at one time there were forty-one in Ohio alone—who traveled about in wagons loaded not only with copies of Thomson's book, but also with lobelia, cayenne, bayberry, poplar bark, and other staples of Thomsonian medicine.

The country's regular doctors could not stop people from swallowing herbal teas, or giving each other herbal enemas. But they did for a time make it hard for anyone to earn his living as a Thomsonian practitioner. "Every medical society in [New York] became virtually a police station, to which resorted spies and informers to communicate evidence for prosecutions," one historian has written. "Many [botanic] practitioners were arrested and fined, many were fined and imprisoned for two months."

The Thomsonians proved, however, to be formidable lobbyists. The

Apparatus for steam-bath treatments, from an 1836 Thomsonian publication

...But the patient died

Samuel Thomson's course of treatment was benign compared to the calomel-and-bleeding methods prescribed by regular physicians. But it, too, could be overdone, as it clearly was in the case of one Jona Sherburn of East Randolph, Vermont, a sufferer from rheumatism.

In the summer of 1841 Sherburn took his pains to Dr. Jehiel Smith, founder and proprietor of the Thomsonian Infirmary and Insane Asylum. Dr. Smith claimed he could cure apoplexy, epilepsy, vertigo, cholera, smallpox and chicken pox, rabies, gout, leprosy, venereal diseases, diabetes, cancer, and rheumatism—to name just a few ailments.

Apparently patient Sherburn did not know of the dubious reputation Dr. Smith had already earned in Strafford, Vermont, twenty miles away. Dr. Smith had left there in 1836—precisely why, no one knows. But before he departed, friends had found it necessary to write testimonials to his character and to attest that they believed "all the evil reports in circulation about him to be entirely false."

Sherburn was admitted to Dr. Smith's hospital on July 19, 1841. Five days later—after prescribed doses of vegetable powder and a ritual of steam baths—he was dead. As a result, the hospital closed abruptly and Dr. Smith disappeared. Sherburn's treatment must have been unusually severe, for the following autopsy was filed by William Nutting, state's attorney for Orange County:

"Head Swelled to Double size.... Blistered in various places. One hand a complete blister, large Blister on one Side. The thighs Blistered, one leg seems parboiled, no feature of the face or body that would be recognised.... Black spots on the Thighs, the inward coats of the Stomach & intestines very much inflamed & some black Spots some parts of the intestines more inflamed than others. a number of Blisters on the inside of the Stomach & intestines.... Stomach & intestines have not any thing in them except the vegetable powder & perhaps a quart of that kind of stuff in the body in all. The inside of the Stomach appears to be seared over as with a hot iron as likewise is the lower parts of the intestines, probably scorched with hot drops or Cayenne pepper...."

—N.B.

New York legislature, for example, could scarcely ignore Samuel Thomson's son John when he arrived at the capitol in Albany with a pro-Thomsonian petition ninety-three feet long that he had personally trundled up State Street in a wheelbarrow. Moreover, the Thomsonians had a big edge over the regular doctors in that their arguments could so easily be elevated to a lofty patriotic plane. Thus Job Haskell, a leading champion of the Thomsonians in the New York legislature, charged that the law prohibiting botanic physicians from accepting fees was an insult to American democracy. "Intrinsic merit, sir," he proclaimed, "is the only qualification which ought to be required of any man to entitle him to practice physic or surgery; it is the only qualification necessary to carry a man from the humblest station under our republican government to the presidential chair." Warming to his work, Haskell spoke feelingly of "the groans and shrieks of the millions who have been destroyed by the lancet and mineral medicines," and gave it as his opinion that "if the awful sounds could burst upon this hall, that law [penalizing botanic practitioners] would be swept with indignation from your statute book...." In the end, such rhetoric was too much for the doctors to withstand, and in state after state, including New York in 1844, all laws regulating the practice of medicine were repealed.

Yet, in the very hour of Thomson's victory over the medical profession, the movement he had founded was beginning to fall apart. One reason was that the patent Thomson had obtained proved ineffective in keeping competitors from stealing his stuff. Other herb doctors, including several former disciples of Thomson's, wrote books offering instruction in modified versions of the Thomsonian system for a fraction of the cost of the *New Guide*. "Shall we not use the herbs of the field," the anonymous author of *The Improved American Family Physician* wanted to know, "without paying Dr. Thomson, or any other man or person, for the use thereof... the sum of twenty dollars?"

Thomson, for his part, angrily accused his imitators not only of stealing his ideas, but of adulterating them as well. Purchasers of Thomsonian rights received a solemn warning that read, in part, "Hold no counsel or advice with... any who shall pretend to have made any improvement on my System of Practice, as I cannot be responsible for the effect of any such improvement. 'Resist the devil, and he will flee from you.'"

Thomson was particularly upset by the ingratitude of some of his former lieutenants, and in 1832, when Thomsonians from all over the country met in convention in Columbus, Ohio, he dwelt on their treachery at some length. "To see persons with whom I have spent days, months, and even years, to instruct them in my hard-earned discoveries, come out against me," he said, "pretending that they are the original discoverers of those things that I have taught them—claiming superiority over me—striving to eclipse the glory of my little star that they saw was beginning to shine, is in my opinion a work too scandalous and mean to pass over without some notice."

The pathos of this appeal appears to have had little effect, for rivals continued to publish books written along Thomsonian lines, and to sell Thomsonian medicines without cutting Thomson in on the profits. Competition was probably inevitable once Thomson's system caught on, but Thomson appears to have swelled the ranks of his competitors by the way he treated his associates. A homely man, with a wide, thin-lipped mouth and deep-set eyes, Thomson was once admiringly described, by the author of a pamphlet called "The Steam Doctor's Defense," as "a peasant from the wild wood shade and isolated scenery of Alstead." According to E. G. House, who claimed to have helped Thomson write his *New Guide to Health*, and who later wrote a book of his own called *The Botanic Family Friend*, Thomson was "an honest man and naturally possessed a good heart." But House also noted that while Thomson was kind to his patients, he had an "uncharitable and morose disposition" and, in his business dealings, had come "under the entire influence of what seem to be his ruling passions, avarice and jealousy." Of the hundreds of agents Thomson had appointed over the years, House wrote, there was "not one as far as our knowledge extends, but what he has denounced as dishonest and unfaithful, and has done all in his power to injure them."

Even followers of Thomson who had no intention of writing books on botanic medicine often came to share House's opinion of their leader. When Thomsonians met in Baltimore in 1834 at their third annual convention, a sympathetic historian has written, there were "heart-burnings smouldering in the bosoms of many.... There was a disposition to resent the claims of Dr. Thomson himself to be the umpire of what was genuine and what was heterodox in the views of others. He was dictatorial of temper and jealous of every individual differing from him or disposed to question his ascendancy."

The collapse of Thomsonianism was also hastened by the insistence of many of the ablest and most energetic Thomsonians, in the face of Samuel Thomson's angry disapproval, that the movement must have medical schools of its own. Some of the heretics were no doubt sincerely persuaded that even the relatively simple rules laid down by Thomson were best applied by practitioners who knew something about physiology and anatomy. "The time is not yet come for every man to be his own physician...," the *Southern Botanic Journal* noted. "As well might you endeavor to make every man his own merchant, his own mechanic, his own lawyer or his own preacher." It is unlikely, however, that Thomson's rebellious followers were moved entirely by concern for their patients. They were also convinced that until they had schools of their own, Thomsonian practitioners would be looked down on by many Americans as ignorant root-and-herb doctors.

Thomson's chief adversary in the fight over the founding of a school was a man named Alva Curtis, who had taken up herbal medicine while teaching at a girls' school in Richmond, Virginia. In 1831, after indiscreetly letting it be known that he was an abolitionist, Curtis had been fired from his job and had moved to Columbus, Ohio, where, three years later, he had become the editor of the most influential of the Thomsonian journals, the *Thomsonian Recorder*. Soon afterward, braving Thomson's wrath, he founded the country's first school of botanic medicine, the Literary and Botanical-Medical Institute of Ohio.

In 1838, at the seventh annual Thomsonian convention, held that year in Philadelphia, Thomson, in effect, excommunicated Curtis, along with his adherents, one of whom was characterized by a spokesman for Thomson as "that ineffable nuisance, that notorious drunken sot, Dr. Draper." The excommunicants, who seem to have been in the majority, thereupon joined together, under Curtis' leadership, to form the Independent Thomsonian Society. Thomson tried to rally his forces by founding a new association, the United States Thomsonian Society, which held one convention, in New York, in 1840. But it showed no further signs of life, and its decease was soon followed by that of Samuel Thomson himself, who died of unspecified causes, in 1843, at the age of seventy-four. According to Nathaniel S. Magoon, a Bostonian who nursed Thomson in his last illness, the old herb doctor's belief in his own medicines never wavered. "Fanatically zealous in his cause," Magoon reported in the *Botanico-Medical Recorder*, "... he passed from life heroically partaking of lobelia, enemas, and the recognized Thomsonian syrups, teas, etc."

Within a few years after Thomson's death even practitioners who stuck closely to his system of therapeutics no longer cared to invoke his name. Curtis and his followers, perhaps believing that they could achieve true respectability only by disowning the unlettered farmer who had set them on the path of botanic medicine, soon dropped the name Independent Thomsonians, choosing instead to call themselves Botanico-Medicals or Physio-Medicals.

But it was to take the country's regular physicians more than fifty years to recover completely from the drubbing Thomson had given them. Millions of Americans went on dosing themselves with herbal remedies and consulting herbal practitioners. Some of these practitioners had picked up their trade on their own, but many were graduates of one of the twenty-odd schools of botanic medicine that were founded in the United States in the nineteenth century. In 1901 a medical historian named Alexander Wilder estimated that several thousand botanic, reformed, physiopathic, and physio-medical doctors were still practicing in the United States. Most of them, according to Wilder, were treating patients pretty much along the lines laid down by Samuel Thomson nearly eighty years before.

Thomson's ideas also unquestionably influenced the founders of the eclectic school of medicine, which flourished in the middle and late years of the century. Most eclectics were graduates of orthodox medical schools, and while they did on occasion prescribe "mineral" medicines, they stuck mainly to vegetable remedies, and eschewed both calomel and the lancet. The first eclectics often went in for heroic botanic medicine, attempting to blast out disease with potent vegetable cathartics. Alexander Wilder, who was himself an eclectic physician, conceded that in the early years of the movement the medicines prescribed by eclectics were "often distasteful and repulsive beyond the power of sensitive patients to endure." But as time went by the eclectics came to rely on inoffensive drugs, and to prescribe them in small quantities, on the sensible theory that often the best thing to do for a sick person was to help him to rest comfortably and, as a leading eclectic physician put it, to keep "the bowels in such restful condition that they would not disturb the patient."

After 1900, herbal medicines lost much of their appeal. Although able to hold their own in competition with calomel, they were completely outclassed by new and rational forms of therapy based on recent discoveries about human physiology and the nature of disease. As L. J. Henderson, a widely respected physiologist and medical sociologist, pointed out some forty years ago, doctors could at long last actually cure people, at least some of the time. "I think it was about 1910 or 1912," Henderson observed, "when it became possible to say of the United States that a random patient with a random disease consulting a doctor chosen at random stood better than a fifty-fifty chance of benefiting from the encounter."

But while most botanic doctors were put out of business by the coming of scientific medicine, the voice of Thomson and his disciples can still be heard, at least faintly, in the land. The notion that simple herbal remedies are inherently superior to the dangerous chemicals prescribed by doctors continues to be given currency by books such as *Back to Eden,* a work described by its publisher as a "million-copy best seller" that came out in 1939 and is still selling briskly in health-food stores. Its subtitle is "The Classic Guide to Herbal Medicine, Natural Foods, and Home Remedies," and its author, Jethro Kloss, devotes a good deal of space to lobelia. Describing Thomson's favorite remedy as "a most efficient relaxant, influencing mucous, serous, nervous, and muscular structures," Kloss recommends its use for the treatment of "coughs, bronchitis, asthma, whooping cough, pneumonia, hysteria, convulsions, suspended animation, tetanus, febrile troubles, etc."

"Lobelia possesses most wonderful properties," Kloss goes on to say. "It is a perfectly harmless relaxant. It loosens disease and opens the way for its elimination from the body. Its action is quick and more effective than radium." Nonpoisonous herbs like lobelia, Kloss concludes, will do everything that conventional doctors try to do with "mercury, antitoxin, serums, vaccines, insulin, strychnine, digitalis, and all [their] poisonous drug preparations...." Samuel Thomson could not have put it better himself.

A free-lance writer, and frequent contributor to this magazine, Spencer Klaw regularly visits a bona fide doctor for checkups.

Preserving a Neighborhood

Saving Hundred-Year-Old Buildings

The idea of urban renewal has traditionally been predicated on the superficially reasonable assumption that the best way to handle crumbling blight is to pluck it out—raze it, tear it down, get rid of it—and build something better: shopping malls and office complexes, say, or apartments and town houses, civic centers and sports arenas.

Yet the careless enthusiasm that has gotten things torn down and built up over the past twenty years or so has inflicted some rather important casualties. Entire neighborhoods have disappeared, neighborhoods that once housed generations of people in that jostling familiarity that gives the city scene its redemptive quality of community. With the neighborhoods went their people; most of them poor or on the thin edge of poverty, they were shuttled off and scattered to whatever housing government might provide or their spindly incomes obtain. And then there were the structures themselves; they spoke of a time when buildings were designed to house people, not institutions, and in their wholesale destruction much was lost of grace, beauty, intricacy, and that sense of continuity that for want of any better term we call history.

So it has gone throughout much of urban America. But not everywhere. Not, for example, in the fifty-six square blocks of the Oak Center district of Oakland, a northern California city situated on the eastern shore of San Francisco Bay. Oak Center was one of the oldest sections of the city. Many of its buildings dated from the Gold Rush period, scores from the 1880's and 1890's, and others from the period immediately following the earthquake and fire of 1906. Once a highly respectable middle-class area, during the years following World War II Oak Center gradually declined, as most such areas did, into an increasingly ignored and all but abandoned urban ghetto, one apparently destined for the bulldozer's blade.

But it remained a neighborhood. When an adjoining area of fifty square blocks was completely razed for redevelopment in 1963, the citizens of Oak Center organized the Oak Center Neighborhood Association, went to the officials of the Oakland Redevelopment Agency (ORA), and made one thing perfectly clear: they wanted to keep their community. Not only keep it, but restore as much of it as they could, give it back some of the history the pressures of the twentieth century had taken from it. In a gesture that defied tradition, the ORA agreed. Thenceforth, rehabilitation and restoration took precedence over simple destruction; no building was demolished if structurally sound; no resident was uprooted who insisted on remaining; and local rights and wishes were given priority. Outright grants of up to $3,500 were made available, as well as twenty-year, 3-per-cent rehabilitation loans of up to $17,400 per living unit. Those who did not wish to restore their homes sold them to the ORA, which refurbished them and sold them to low-income families at down payments as small as $200 and with mortgages running from twenty to forty years.

The pressures of recession recently brought the Oak Center experiment to an end, but not before more than 350 out of the 465 salvageable buildings in the district had been completely restored. Its citizens hope to obtain funding in the future to complete the remaining work. One would like to think they can, for in Oak Center the concept of urban renewal has acquired perhaps a more precise meaning: the renewal and preservation not only of some fine old buildings—as the photographs taken by Chad Slattery on these and the following two pages illustrate—but of one of the oldest and best of American urban traditions—the neighborhood.   —T. W.

Looming like the haunted house of everyone's dream, the "Queen Anne" Victorian on the opposite page stood for nearly a century as the symbol of a neighborhood's past. Structurally unsound, it was eventually razed. The inverted teardrop window above was lovingly restored to provide an elegant touch to another home.

"...the truest record of life as it was lived in the world yesterday..."

These photographs are a living demonstration of the spirit of Frank Lloyd Wright's observation: "What is architecture anyway? Is it the vast collection of the various buildings which have been built to please the varying taste of the various lords of mankind? I think not. No, I know that architecture is life; or at least it is life itself taking form and therefore it is the truest record of life as it was lived in the world yesterday, as it is lived today or ever will be lived." The people of Oak Center who chose to defy the wrecker's ball may not have been familiar with Wright's dictum, but they would know what he meant. The row of houses directly above, boarded up pending restoration; the fully restored houses on the right; and all of the intricate pediments and cornices on the opposite page— these are more than houses or parts of houses. They are statements that help define what it must have been like to live here two generations ago—and what it can still be like for those among us stubborn enough to believe that the human scale of the urban neighborhood is a value the twentieth century had better preserve.

108

109

POSTSCRIPTS TO HISTORY

LINCOLN'S PURPLE PERIOD, OR, WE'RE GLAD HE GOT IT OUT OF HIS SYSTEM

The future President strikes a suitably stiff oratorical pose at the time of the Lincoln-Douglas debates of 1858.
LIBRARY OF CONGRESS

Abraham Lincoln is generally considered to have been the best writer of all our Presidents. But like any other writer, it took him a while to get there. As an example, we offer the following excerpt from remarks he delivered to the Illinois House of Representatives on December 26, 1839, a speech that derived its emotional character from the dire conviction that Van Buren Democrats might ultimately bring ruin to the Republic. In his conclusion, the thirty-year-old Whig became nearly unhinged:

"I know that the great volcano at Washington, aroused and directed by the evil spirit that reigns there, is belching forth the lava of political corruption, in a current broad and deep, which is sweeping with frightful velocity over the whole length and breadth of the land, bidding fair to leave unscathed no green spot or living thing, while on its bosom are riding like demons on the waves of Hell, the imps of that evil spirit, and fiendishly taunting all those who dare resist its destroying course, with the hopelessness of their effort; and knowing this, I cannot deny that all may be swept away. Broken by it, I, too, may be; bow to it I never will. The *probability* that we may fall in the struggle *ought not* to deter us from the support of a cause we believe to be just; it *shall not* deter me. If ever I feel the soul within me elevate and expand to those dimensions not wholly unworthy of its Almighty Architect, it is when I contemplate the cause of my country, deserted by all the world beside, and I standing up boldly and alone and hurling defiance at her victorious oppressors. . . ."

FLAGRANT MISUSE OF FLAG FLOGGED

The cover of our February, 1977, issue inspired, among others, the following letter from the Honorable Thomas F. Butt, probate judge of the Thirteenth Chancery Court of the State of Arkansas:

"Surely, surely, your make-up staff reversed the negative on the reproduction photo of Speaker Joe Cannon. Surely 'Uncle Joe' was not left-handed; surely, the national flag behind the speaker was not incorrectly hung, in actuality. Properly hung, the starred union of the flag should be at its upper right quarter rather than in the upper left quarter as shown in the photo. I suspect this letter will be about the 4,004th such communication inviting your attention to this apparent error."

Although we received considerably fewer than 4,004 such letters, there were, indeed, many of them. Actually, we can provide a bit of information that most people apparently do not know (and that we did not know until we looked into it): before 1942, there was no uniform official code for the proper display of the flag. Until then, within Congress and out (as the photograph on pages 74–75 of this issue will demonstrate), the national emblem tended to be hung every which way, with few people being overly concerned about it. (Note, however, that if the flag in the Cannon photograph were turned counterclockwise to hang horizontally, the field of stars would be in its accustomed position.) Whether "Uncle Joe" normally held the gavel in his left hand is not known, but to corroborate our conviction that the picture on our cover was not reversed, we point out that his coat is buttoned in the manner that has been fashionable among men for generations.

HAIR-RAISING ANTIQUITY

In "Who Invented Scalping?" an article in our April, 1977, issue, James Axtell argued that—contrary to recent revisionist notions—Europeans did not teach the Indians how to scalp. The Indians, he said, had learned it all by themselves and had practiced it long before Europeans inflicted themselves on this innocent continent. Additional evidence to support Mr. Axtell's theory has since come to us from Douglas Owsley and Hugh Berryman, anthropologists at the University of Tennessee, who furnished us with the photograph above and a description of what happened to the skull's former owner:

"The human skull shown in the picture is that of an adult male American Indian who was scalped. The bones of this individual [who died in about A.D. 1300] were recovered during an archaeological excavation of the Arnold site in Williamson County, Tennessee.... Cuts in the bone (visible in the photograph) extend across the forehead in the approximate location of the hairline. Two or three strokes with a sharp stone knife were all that was required.

"In the historic period, and likely the prehistoric as well, certain tribes in the southeastern United States considered the scalp symbolic of an individual's soul. Loss of the scalp had supernaturally dangerous consequences to the victim's eternal future unless his death was avenged by friends and relatives."

MATERIA HYSTERICA

The twitches, convulsions, and erratic behavior of the seventeenth-century Salem, Massachusetts, girls who accused their elders of witchcraft have been the subject of speculation for nearly three hundred years. It is still not known why they acted as they did, but theories continue to abound—including a unique recent one, which enjoyed a short vogue before it was shoveled into the dustbin of the unlikely.

The new theory was developed by Linda Caporeal, a graduate student in psychology at the University of California at Santa Barbara. In the April 2, 1976, issue of *Science* magazine, she argued that the Salem girls behaved in a crazed fashion because they had ingested ergot, a parasitic fungus that grows on rye, a staple in colonial New England. Convulsive ergotism, a condition caused by the long-term consumption of ergot, manifests itself in symptoms remarkably similar to those displayed by the afflicted Salem girls: hallucinations, vertigo, headaches, crawling sensations on the skin, and painful muscular contractions resulting in vomiting, diarrhea, and convulsions.

To support this theory, Caporeal marshaled considerable evidence. The 1691 growing season, she pointed out, had been warm and rainy, ideal conditions for the parasite's infestation of the rye crop. All the afflicted girls probably were fed rye obtained from the same fields to the west of Salem Village. And, Caporeal noted, the hysteria ended abruptly after the harvesting of the 1692 rye crop, which had grown in a season of drought and hence was less susceptible to ergot infestation.

Caporeal's dramatic notion was hardly advanced, however, before it was refuted. In the past several months a number of articles have appeared in learned journals taking her to task. It seems that convulsive ergotism occurs only in individuals suffering vitamin A deficiencies. In healthy people, the fungus does not produce hallucinations and hysteria; it produces a form of gangrene. Since vitamin A is found primarily in fish and dairy products, and since Salem Village was a farming community bordering a major seaport, it seems unlikely that adolescent girls from reasonably prosperous families would have suffered this deficiency. Had ergotism been the devil's tool in the small New England village, putrefaction, not execution, would more likely have resulted.

PRONOUNCE IT "PEWTOWN," SON

Grace Lichtenstein's article, "Pronounce it Callaradda, Son" (October, 1976), inspired a letter from Mr. J. Leslie Tooher of Schenectady, New York:

"Your article states that Pueblo, Colorado, is pronounced 'Pee-eh-blo' by residents. This comes as a surprise. I was born in Pueblo around the turn of the century and it was my home until 1923. To my best recollection, I never heard it pronounced any way other than 'Pwe'blo' or 'Pye'blo' (both 'e's being short). Moreover, it is interesting to recall that among the city's industries, there were then two smelters and a steel-producing plant. When the wind was 'right,' the smelter-smoke, soot, and other stenches made life in general unbearable, thus the appellation of 'Pewtown' enjoyed wide popularity."

RELIEF FOR TIRED EYES

A number of readers have written us to celebrate the fact that we have lately taken to running our articles all in a piece, rather than "jumping" them to the back of the issue. Apparently many people appreciate not being forced to rummage around in the lost-and-found region of the back pages, and we plan to continue this new policy whenever possible.

Solution to the April Crossword Puzzle

THE FOUNDING PHYSICIANS

The article on the founding of the Johns Hopkins medical complex that ran in our February, 1976, issue generated some interesting mail. Dr. Ronald Rosenthal of Nashville, Tennessee, writes:

"On page 30 you have a reproduction of the famous portrait by John Singer Sargent of the four founding physicians of this great institution. Unfortunately, you have Dr. Halsted and Dr. Osler reversed; in the portrait Dr. Halsted is standing directly to the left of Dr. Welch, and Dr. Osler is sitting directly to the right of Dr. Kelly. You are calling Osler Halsted, and Halsted Osler. Friends of mine at Johns Hopkins say that during the painting of the portrait Mr. Sargent became so incensed at Dr. Halsted over one thing or another that when it came time to paint Halsted's picture, he used inferior pigments so that Halsted's face would fade more rapidly than the others. I have no idea whether this story is true or not; certainly in the portrait Halsted is in somewhat of a shadow as compared to the other three."

Dr. Stephen Lehrer of New York City called our attention to an article in the *Journal of the American Medical Association* which indicates that the unfortunate Dr. Halsted was not cured of his narcotic addiction before he came to Baltimore. In the late 1890's Dr. Osler wrote a private biographical sketch of his colleague. In it he said:

"When we recommended [Halsted] as full surgeon to the Hospital in 1890, I believed, and Welch did too, that he was no longer addicted to morphia. He had worked so well and so energetically that it did not seem possible that he could take the drug and do so much.

"About six months after the full position had been given, I saw him in a severe chill, and this was the first intimation I had that he was still taking morphia. Subsequently I had many talks about it and gained his full confidence. He had never been able to reduce the amount to less than three grains daily; on this he could do his work comfortably and maintain his excellent physical vigor (for he was a very muscular fellow). I do not think that anyone suspected him, not even Welch."

But Osler appended a footnote to this many years later that suggests that Halsted did finally triumph over his addiction:

"Subsequently, 10 Jan. 1898, he got the amount down to 1½ grains, and of late years (1912) has possibly got on without it."